Meditations
for the
Road Warrior

Meditations for the Road Warrior

Mark Sanborn
and Terry Paulson,
editors

Baker Books

A Division of Baker Book House Co
Grand Rapids, Michigan 49516

Published by Baker Books
a division of Baker Book House Company
P.O. Box 6287, Grand Rapids, MI 49516-6287

Second printing, November 1998

Printed in the United States of America

Library of Congress Cataloging-in-Publication Data

Meditations for the road warrior / Mark Sanborn, Terry Paulson, editors.
    p.   cm.
Includes index.
ISBN 0-8010-1172-8
    1. Businesspeople—Prayer-books and devotions—English. 2. Travelers—Prayer-books and devotions—English.
I. Sanborn, Mark. II. Paulson, Terry L.
BV4596.B8M43 1998
242—dc21   98-17859

A portion of the editors' royalties will go to Gideons International for their mission of placing Bibles in hotel rooms.

For information about academic books, resources for Christian leaders, and all new releases available from Baker Book House, visit our web site:
    http://www.bakerbooks.com

Contents

Preface   9
Introduction   11

Above the Clouds . . . the Sun Is Always Shining!
Admiral Club Card Holder
Am I Weary?
Ambassadors for the Kingdom
Anybody There?
As the Eagles Fly
An Attitude of Gratitude
Be Prepared
A Body on Loan from God
Brother, Can You Spare Me a Dime?
Childlike Wonder
Curse of the Middle Seat
Desires Fulfilled
Destination: Eternity's Gate
Dirty Corners
Do You Pray like You Pack?
Doing Good Work
Easier on the Road
ET Phone Home
Far from Blameless
The Faster I Go, the More Behind I Get
Fear No Evil
Fear Not
The Fight

Contents

Finding Peace in the Midst of Anxiety
First Class Service
Gate 34, Gate 32, or the Narrow Gate?
Get Out That Road Map!
Getting a Bigger Picture
The God of All Circumstances
Going Home
The Good in All Things
Good News from Afar
The Greatest of These
Holding Forth the Word of Life
Honors Bestowed—the Journey Rewarded
If This Is Tuesday, I Must Be in Cleveland
The Importance of Looking Up
In Search of True Riches
Insight from an In-flight Magazine
Integrity on the Road
It Won't Matter Then
I've Got More Ribbons than You!
The Joy of Litter
Keep Swimming
A Lamp to My Feet
Lasting Glory
A Letter to My Son
Letting Go and Letting God
Listening to the Still, Small Voice
Living Boldly
The Long and Grateful Road
Love Away from Home
Loving Enemies You Meet on the Road
Making Time
Meeting the Messiah Today
Of Wine and Witness
Oh, the Tongue!

Okay, Where's the Lesson?
On the Road Again—Wearing a Pink Ribbon
On Wings of Eagles
An Open Seat to Peace
The Painful Process
Perilous Times
The Pilot
A Prayer Meant to Be Sung
Price for Privilege
A Purpose for Every Trip
Put Your Luggage Where Your Faith Is
Raisin Bran or . . . Lovely Thoughts!
Rent That Cart!
The Resort of Solitude
Road Rage and Unexpected Blessings
Seeing through God's Eyes
Seizing the Day for Joy
The Shepherd Cares for His Sheep
Some Suffering Optional
Someone Is Watching
Standing at the Crossroad
Strange Parking Lots, Dark Streets, Long Hallways
The Sun
Supernatural Horizon
Supreme Sacrifice
Sweet Fellowship
Taking a Daily Leap for Joy
Tears and Prayers for a Stranger
Temple Maintenance
Thirsty
Too Busy
Trading In My TV Party
Traveler's Alert

Contents

Traveling Companions
Truth-Centered Living on the Road
An Unknown Soldier Goes Home
Upgrade to First Class
What a Deal I Have for You!
What Do I Have to Offer?
Whistle while You Work
Who Are You Praying For?
Worshiping with Those Other Christians

About the Editors   115
Contributors   117
Index   121

8

Preface

The flight attendant and I were talking about our kids. My son was five months old at the time. Her children were in their teens. There is always a bond between parents born out of the challenges of loving and raising kids. We also had something else in common: We both traveled for a living. She asked what type of work I was in. I explained that I was a professional speaker and author. "What do you talk and write about?" she wanted to know. I had the manuscript for *Meditations for the Road Warrior* in my briefcase, so I showed it to her. She asked if she could read some of it before we landed, and I told her I'd be glad to share it with her.

From where I was sitting, I could see her reaction to the manuscript. I had no idea what her spiritual beliefs were, but her excitement was obvious. The more she read, the more animated she became. The words seemed to connect with her. At one point she jumped up to show another flight attendant. He read a few pages, and before landing, he put an encouraging hand on my shoulder and told me how important he thought the book was.

At that point, before the book had even been published, I knew our work had not been in vain. That day I had a glimpse of the reaction we hope the book creates when it reaches the hands of you, our reader.

Terry and I, and the other contributors to this book, share two things in common: We travel extensively and, most importantly, we love our Lord. My co-editor and I brought together a committed team of traveling Christians to write this book because of a need we knew existed from personal experience. How do people face the unique challenges of living out their faith while they are on the road and away from family, friends, and church? All of us knew the challenges and had even worked out some solutions. God led us to share with you some of what we've learned on our journeys as Christian Road Warriors.

The meditations in this book are personal. Some were written out of joy, others out of pain. Behind some meditations are stories of victory; behind others are stories of disappointments and setbacks. But they all express a profound need to come to terms with the most important issue of life, especially as that issue affects the traveler: How do we live to honor our Creator?

You may never meet any of us, but that's okay because how the messages affect your spiritual growth is far more important than any of the messengers. Our sincere hope is that our words encourage, comfort, and sometimes challenge you as you travel. Most importantly, we hope these words assist you in developing a deeper, richer relationship with your heavenly Father and his Son, Jesus Christ. There is nothing in this life or the next more important than that.

Mark Sanborn

Introduction

Subject: I Love You and Miss You
From: God2@heaven.com (Jesus Christ)
To: RoadWarrior@childofGod.com

I never thought I'd have to reach you this way, but I wanted to make sure you would read this so you would know how much I love and care for you. Yesterday, I saw you racing through the terminal. I heard you laughing and talking with the ticket agent when you arrived with time to spare. I had hoped that as soon as you'd settled into your seat on the plane, you'd want to talk with me too. So as your plane took off to your next destination, I painted a glorious sunset to close your day. I don't think you even looked. You were already busy with your computer. I even seated you next to another Christian, but little was said—so few words and nothing about me. I waited. You didn't bless your meal. You didn't call on me, but I just kept on loving you.

As you waited for your hotel shuttle, I saw you glancing at your watch. I felt your frustration. I wanted to touch you and calm you. I spilled moonlight onto your face and supplied a refreshing, warm breeze. At the hotel, there was barely time to unpack your clothes and gobble down your mint. I thought maybe you would reach for my Word in the drawer, but instead you glanced at the news while you scanned your agenda for your next day's meeting. You didn't even think of me. I wanted so much to comfort and center you. I wanted you to come near to me so I could show you I was there to love you.

The next day, you woke up with just enough time to shower, dress, and pack. When you left the hotel, I exploded a brilliant sunrise into a glorious morning for you. I threw the vibrant colors of spring flowers across your path. A chorus of birds orchestrated a litany of morning love songs. As a child you used to notice but seldom now. I fear I'm like a flight attendant giving safety instructions to a plane full of road warriors so engrossed in their own world that they don't even hear the lifesaving information I provide for them. You did find time for coffee and the paper, but you were off again before you could even feel my presence. Did you really think that what was happening in your world was more important than what was happening in your relationship with me? I loved you anyway.

My love for you is richer than any account you could land, and your need for me is greater than any entry on your to do list. But I fear that outside of a direct miracle there is no way I can get placed on your busy agenda.

Father sends his love; he cares too. Fathers are just that way. So, please, call on me soon in any way that suits you. Don't be afraid to call collect; the Holy Spirit is ready to accept the charges. No matter how long it takes, I'll keep trying to connect—because I love you.

Your Friend, Savior, and Lord,
Jesus

Would it take an e-mail from Jesus to get your attention? Do you struggle with ways to find time to strengthen your faith in your hectic life as a productive road warrior? If your answer is yes, you're not alone, and help is on the way.

This book contains a collection of targeted and timely devotional messages from professional speakers, authors, and fellow Christians who share your journey. They are spiritual road warriors who can speak to your world, because it is their world. Each short message is designed to challenge you, uplift you, and help connect you to God's power while you're on the road. May you enjoy reading these messages as much as we enjoyed compiling them.

Above the Clouds . . . the Sun Is Always Shining!

For the L ord God is a sun and shield; The L ord gives grace and glory; No good thing does He withhold from those who walk uprightly. O L ord of hosts, How blessed is the man who trusts in Thee! Psalm 84:11–12 NASB

As I hurry onto the plane, my travel bag is filled with correspondence, seminar materials, slides, and books. My mind is filled with should's, ought to's, and will do's for this three-hour flight. My soul is crowded with concerns for family, friends, business, and travel complexities.

I pull the blind to shut out the strong heat of the Phoenix runway, turn on the overhead light, prop a pillow in the unexplained concavity of my uncomfortable seat, and prepare to work during my airborne journey. Intent! Intense! Stressed!

And then . . . breakfast is served! It is a temporary respite from my self-imposed busyness. With a sudden curiosity to see what the ground looks like, I open the shade. Expecting to see some type of scenery, I instead find myself floating on an incredibly beautiful blanket of white, puffy clouds. Above these clouds I see the most beautiful sunrise imaginable with hues of pink, yellow, and orange against a clear blue sky. Above the clouds, yes, the sun is always shining.

And he is our sun—the Son of God!

He is our purpose for travel—the journey is his.

He is our reason for the business of life—the plans are his.

He is our peace amid the heaviness of our soul.

He is the relief from the ground below.

He is our Son!

 Lord, thank you for heavenly perspective above the clouds, for earthly toils beneath.

Naomi Rhode

Admiral Club Card Holder

And the city was pure gold. Revelation 21:18 NASB

I rush to gate 33 in the Dallas airport, take the elevator up one floor, and present my Admiral Club Card to a hostess, who then lets me enter the club. It is a haven for the busy, tired traveler—a quiet, peaceful, restful, gracious respite from the hassle of connecting flights, busy schedules, and stressed travelers.

What a privilege to be here, Lord. Thank you. Now a million mile traveler with American Airlines, I have a lifetime membership in this club. Possessing a lifetime Admiral Club Card guarantees me access to this special club whenever I travel. I love partaking of the perks of passage.

But then what?—I look into your Word and smile!

How easy it is to focus on today's rest stops and forget the eternal home you have prepared . . . before the foundations of the world. A place where the very streets will be paved with gold. A place of rest, peace, joy, perspective, redemption, and the ultimate in celebration. All because you came to "prepare a place for us" through the redemption available through belief in your Son.

I am so thrilled to be a card holder—a card holder of your "Admiral Club," to be guaranteed eternity with you.

Lord, help me to have the guidance of your Holy Spirit to introduce new members to your "Admiral Club" as I travel on my journey. Instead of keeping the club to myself, help me to tell others of this eternal haven of peace, rest, and eternal joy with Jesus.

Naomi Rhode

Am I Weary?

But as for you, brethren, do not grow weary in doing good.
2 Thessalonians 3:13 NKJV

Fatigue, n. 1. labor; 2. weariness or exhaustion from labor, exertion, or stress." As a road warrior, it seems as though I'm always busy. If I'm not busy traveling, I'm busy trying to arrange another reason to travel. As with most road warriors, travel is where the action of our lives finds its meaning . . . and its draining fatigue.

Yes, we tire physically, mentally, and even emotionally. We tire to the point at which we question our sanity, we doubt our ability to go on, or we are even tempted to use alcohol or drugs to blunt the pain. At this point in time, I turn to my spiritual strength, which knows no weariness. Turning it all over to the Lord, I do as Jesus said: "But when you pray, go into your most private room, and closing the door, pray to your Father Who is in secret; and your Father Who sees in secret will reward you in the open" (Matt. 6:6 AMP).

Then the earthly fatigue in my bones cannot overwhelm the tumultuous joy in my heart, and once again my spirit soars. The joy of my faith does not come from the TV sitcom that drones from my hotel room; it comes from within when I let go and let God lift me up and guide me through another day.

Dear Lord, my God-given spirit is alive and crackling with gratitude for the love and care you bestow on me. I can do the footwork knowing that my Savior is at the wheel.

Bob Sherer

Ambassadors for the Kingdom

Jesus said, "My kingdom is not of this world. . . . My kingdom is from another place." John 18:36

An ambassador to a foreign country represents his homeland. As Christians, we are no longer "of this world," although we still reside in it. Along with accepting Christ and the promise of eternal citizenship in the kingdom of God comes the realization that we won't truly be home until we leave this earthly existence. In the meantime, we live here on earth as ambassadors of God.

It is a privilege to represent the living God. But there is an old question I'm sure you've heard before: "If you were arrested for being a Christian, would there be enough evidence to convict you?" What substantive differences in your life can others see that would make them want to "relocate" to the kingdom of heaven, which you represent?

Sometimes ambassadors lose their positions of honor. They do something to disgrace their country and are called home, or they offend their country of residence and are expelled. Although our eternal inheritance is secure in Christ, we can still disgrace the King through wrongful behavior.

But those good things we do—in our work, with our families, and in our relationships with those we encounter in our travels—are a credit to our King. When we serve as worthy ambassadors, God is honored.

Are we leading people to or driving them away from the kingdom?

Lord, I want to serve you with honor. Remind me that I represent an eternal kingdom and that the things I do reflect not only on my personal integrity but on you, whom I serve. I pray that you will equip me to be a worthy ambassador for you.

Mark Sanborn

Anybody There?

He who has ears, let him hear. Matthew 11:15

While in the hotel business center, I watched with amusement as an excited grandmother sent her very first fax to someone back home. She was so in awe of the "newfangled" technology and having such a good time with it that she wanted to send another one just for the fun of it. When she received an immediate reply to her fax, her enthusiasm knew no bounds. She left exclaiming, "Oh! This is so wonderful!"

While waiting for my own fax to go through, I couldn't help but think, "Wouldn't it be wonderful if God had a fax machine? He could just fax me his messages!" My thoughts were interrupted by a man telling me that my message was not being received. Something was wrong on the other end.

I left feeling frustrated. I was also sobered by the thought that my heavenly Father must also experience that same feeling. His messages are all around me, and yet how many times do I miss them because the ears of my heart have been turned off to his voice. Maybe I don't receive his words because I get so busy with other messages that seem more important . . . or maybe I simply choose to ignore them. Whatever the reason, one thing is certain: Even if God did have a fax machine, it still wouldn't work if the "receiver" were turned off.

Father, forgive me for all the times I have missed your messages. I know that if I would just listen, I would hear your voice. Tune my heart and ears today so that I will not only receive your message but respond with obedience.

Gail Wenos

As the Eagles Fly

Those who wait on the LORD shall renew their strength; They shall mount up with wings like eagles. Isaiah 40:31 NKJV

It was raining when we left. Heavy, thick clouds rolling across the field made a charcoal day even darker. Damp cold seeped through the jetway as we shuffled in gloomy silence into the plane. The weather matched my mood. The meeting hadn't gone the way I had hoped. What had gone wrong? Had it been the early morning lethargy of the group? My lack of concentration? Perhaps I needed more stringent preparation? Maybe I'm just not cut out for this profession?

And then the plane took off, carrying us all higher and higher until the dazzling brilliance of the sun's glare streamed into the cabin. How could I have forgotten? In looking at the dark of the minute, I had forgotten the ever present presence of the sun transcending the rain-soaked clouds.

Just as I had forgotten about the sun's radiance, it's easy to forget that God's Son is always there to push beyond our feelings of failure so we can experience his grace and affirming presence. Once again, I nailed the heavy weight of my doubts and fears to the cross and, on the strength of his wings, soared.

Lord, help me to learn from the dark and look for the light and, in so doing, grow and go where you desire.

Eileen McDargh

An Attitude of Gratitude

In every thing give thanks: for this is the will of God in Christ Jesus concerning you. 1 Thessalonians 5:18 KJV

A wealthy Christian businessman, who had given over half of his income to the church, shared some of his wisdom with me. He said if a person had a roof over his head, clothes on his back, food in his stomach, and good health, he should be very thankful. Growing up during the depression, this man could speak with authority.

Years ago on a business trip, I visited several small towns in the Southwest. I can remember one town in particular where I had to spend two nights. There were only two little run-down hotels in the town. I tried to pick what appeared to be the better of the two. I must have made a mistake.

Upon opening the door to my room, I immediately noticed the twenty-year-old shag, or was it rag, carpet. There were spots where spills of one kind or another had discolored and matted the carpet fibers. There was also a hint of animal odor that would occasionally twinge my nose. The bed squeaked, the sink dripped, and the toilet paper was industrial strength thickness and texture. Yes, these are the experiences from which great stories grow.

Then I remembered the words of my old friend, and I remembered to be thankful for a roof over my head, food in my stomach, clothes on my back, and my good health. Living with an attitude of gratitude keeps us thankful for the simple things.

Lord, I come to you with a heart of thankfulness and gratitude for the many blessings I have. You are the supplier of all that I need. Thank you for my home, my physical sustenance, my clothing, and my health.

George Hendley

Be Prepared

Always be prepared to give an answer to everyone who asks you to give the reason for the hope that you have. But do this with gentleness and respect. 1 Peter 3:15

I had just finished speaking at an association's annual meeting when two of the audience members approached me. One of them said, "In your speech you said you've found most people can't come up with a definite answer when you ask them why they get out of bed in the morning. So what gets you out of bed in the morning?"

I began my answer with, "I'm a Christian . . ." Even as I said it, I realized how vague that is to many people. Does it mean I'm religious? That I believe in Jesus? Or is it cultural, as in a nation built on Judeo-Christian values?

Jesus Christ was very clear on what it meant to be a Christian when he invited some common fishermen to follow him. The apostles did more than believe; they followed.

". . . and I believe the purpose of life is to know God and honor him," I finished. It was the most complete yet concise answer I could give for that weighty question.

Being able to explain rationally and sincerely why we believe in Christ is one of the surest ways to have eternal influence on the lives of those we encounter on the road. How ready are you to provide an answer the next time somebody asks?

Lord, if someone asks me what I believe, help me to explain my faith. Help me to make time for study and thought so that I may be a more effective defender of the faith and eternal influencer of others for you.

Mark Sanborn

A Body on Loan from God

They will run and not grow weary, they will walk and not be faint.
Isaiah 40:31

Your body is on loan from God. Taking time to exercise brings more than health and the development of self-control. It is a time for reflection, a prayer in motion. When going on the road, two of the first things I pack are my running shorts and my jogging shoes. Now, when the Olympics came to Los Angeles, the gold medal was quite safe. I've seen myself run; there are as many people ahead of me as there are behind. I run for T-shirts and health, not gold medals. But when I'm on the road, give me an open trail and good weather, and I'm off for a run. Jogging keeps my body and mind healthy and flexible.

Like the spiritual jogging involved in regular prayer and daily devotions, regular exercise becomes a positive addiction that prepares our bodies for action. To be used by God, we are called to be ready, spiritually and physically. You ask, "Who ever heard of Jesus running?" Well, who ever heard of Jesus driving a car or taking an elevator? Jesus worked and walked his way through life. While we work to take effort out of our lives, God calls us to responsible use of our bodies. A prescription worth remembering is "Use it or lose it!"

Lord, help me to take care of my body so I am better able to serve you. Help me to find the right exercise and the time to make it a habit I can live with.

Terry Paulson

23

Brother, Can You Spare Me a Dime?

Whoever trusts in his riches will fall. Proverbs 11:28

Unfortunately, my wife didn't have time to make it to the airport. It may be a small world, but not if you have to make a thirty-seven-mile trip during an L.A. morning rush hour. I again checked through my luggage, my pants, and my jacket. My earlier assessment was accurate: I had no wallet, no money clip, and no driver's license, and I was thirty-five minutes away from getting on a plane for Minneapolis. There would be taxi drivers to pay and ticket agents who would want to see my smiling face on a California license. I was used to being a self-sufficient and experienced road warrior, but now it was my turn to need some help.

I decided to see what unique answers God might provide to handle the poor hand I'd dealt myself. So I endured the extensive luggage inspection for travelers without I.D., trusted my wife to come up with a creative way to get money to me, and took off on an adventure. Time and time again that day, I was blessed by the trust and hospitality people showed me on my journey. I kept hearing the words of Jesus recorded in Luke 12:31–32: "Set your heart on his kingdom, and your food and drink will come as a matter of course. Don't be afraid" (PHILLIPS).

I, like many road warriors, have been cursed by the illusion of self-sufficiency only to be humbled and blessed by the need to let others serve me.

 Lord, thank you for letting me know that I don't have to do it all myself and for replacing my worry with wonder.

Terry Paulson

Childlike Wonder

Truly I say to you, whoever does not receive the kingdom of God like a child shall not enter it at all. Mark 10:15 NASB

I love looking at clouds and fields and mountains from planes. After twenty years of flying, it still thrills me. Clouds are my favorites, next to mountains, that is. Being from Michigan and doing most of my traveling in the inside two thirds of America, I've trained myself not to long for mountains.

I marvel at what God has molded with his feathery, fluffy clay. A crocodile eating a palm tree! Whole!! An upside-down elephant floating on an inner tube!

As fascinating as clouds are to me, it's even more of a wonder to me why so many business travelers have grown cold to anything but work. They don't look out the window even when passing over the Rocky Mountains! I can hardly write that sentence without screaming. Some travelers won't smile, many barely say hi, and most get irate at any sound that seems to be coming from a child.

I'm not crazy about crying babies myself except that they remind me of another of God's great miracles. Plus, my heart goes out to so many parents patiently traveling with fussy kids. Talk about courage and energy.

My own three children continually teach me that life and the world around us are so full of flowers to smell, things to laugh about, water balloons to throw, someone to tickle, and sunsets to ooh and aah over.

Dear God, I'm not going to let any more grumpy travelers in the seat next to me steal my joy when I show them the monkey riding the missile across the sky.

Bill Sanders

Curse of the Middle Seat

In his heart a man plans his course, but the Lord determines his steps.
Proverbs 16:9

I'm sorry. We have a full load today. The only seats available are middle seats." With those words, my mood went into a severe decline, taking my attitude with it. The middle seat! I hate the middle seat!

By the time I had settled into my cramped quarters, my attitude had hit rock bottom. "Lord," I whined, "please open up a more comfortable seat." His answer? The plane took off with me still sitting unhappily in the middle.

As the lady next to me began a conversation, I thought, "Oh, great! Not only am I stuck with the middle seat, but now I have a talkative seatmate as well!"

You can imagine my surprise to find that as the conversation continued, our small talk gave way to a seriousness resulting in a willingness on the woman's part to open her heart to Jesus Christ. It was then that I realized I was sitting right where God wanted me all along.

How amazed and humbled I felt to know that my heavenly Father had used me in spite of me. I had been so concerned about my own comfort that I had almost missed his assignment. No longer will I fight the curse of the middle seat, because I now know that it can be a seat of blessing instead.

Father, forgive me when I become so self-absorbed and concerned about my own comfort. Give me a new focus so that when I face times of discomfort, I will be able to see opportunities for blessings.

Gail Wenos

Desires Fulfilled

Trust in the LORD and do good; dwell in the land and enjoy safe pasture. Delight yourself in the LORD and he will give you the desires of your heart. Psalm 37:3–4

Delight yourself in the LORD and he will give you the desires of your heart." What an amazing verse! But what do our hearts desire? I can think of a lot of desires that frankly God wouldn't want to give me and that I would not benefit from.

Maybe that's why the passage begins with an admonishment to first delight in the Lord. When we delight in him, our action produces a change of heart and brings our desires into alignment with what delights him. When we seek the heart of God, his heart becomes our heart.

Think of the things you desired before you became a Christian and consider the changes that took place in your life as you learned from the Word, godly teaching, and fellowship with other believers. One of the highest objectives of Christian growth must be knowing and pursuing the heart of God.

When we travel, we have goals to achieve and a job to do. We want to succeed in our work. Seeking the heart of God can become secondary. The challenge is to put God first in everything we do, including our travels. Then we can bring our hearts into alignment with his. Once that happens, we have opened the floodgates of his blessings.

Lord, check the desires of my heart to make sure they are pleasing to you. Plant what you desire deep within me, and remind me to keep you first wherever I am.

Mark Sanborn

Destination: Eternity's Gate

For God so loved the world, that he gave his only begotten Son, that whosoever believeth in him should not perish, but have everlasting life. John 3:16 KJV

Houston, gate 6; Minneapolis, gate 10; Phoenix, gate 31A," the flight attendant articulately announces. We travelers listen alertly, anxious not to miss the next segment of our important journey. Our vision is acutely focused, our legs primed to run if necessary.

How the Lord must smile in amusement as he watches us scurry through the maze of endless airports, car rentals, cabs, trolleys, elevators, escalators . . . all transporting us to our "urgent" destination, only to do it all again in a day or two or three! How easy to be caught up in the "tyranny of the urgent," a phrase I heard years ago, and to miss the meaning of the moment and the perspective of God's plan.

And then the realization of our eternal destination echoes in our souls. The gate is narrow, the time of departure uncertain, the journey inevitable, and the price already paid. Free—paid by the blood of his only Son. Available—first class seating if we will only believe in him. Safe—destination guaranteed, eternity with our Lord Jesus Christ.

Oh, Father, thank you for the price you paid for my eternal destination—heaven. Slow me down, focus my thoughts on you, and sanctify my purposes with your guidance.

Naomi Rhode

Dirty Corners

Cleanse me with hyssop, and I will be clean; wash me, and I will be whiter than snow. Psalm 51:7

The room *looked* clean at first glance, but a closer inspection revealed areas that had been missed by housekeeping. The wastebasket was still full; a used washcloth hung on the tub; a dirty fork was next to the telephone.

My comfort level took a nose dive. Even though the rest of the room *looked* clean, I began to have questions. Are the sheets clean? Have those towels been used? I just couldn't be sure. The room now *felt* dirty.

It only took one phone call to housekeeping to remedy the situation, and this time I *knew* the room was clean because I was there when they cleaned it! How good it felt to *know* it was clean!

Looking around with a feeling of satisfaction, I realized that this must be how my heavenly Father feels when I allow him to clean out those hidden corners of my life. My body is his residence, and I know he doesn't want to live in a heart that is dirty.

I'm so thankful he lets me know when things are not right, and with loving patience he waits for me to ask him for his cleansing. As I earnestly cry out, "Cleanse me, oh, God," he does just that. How good it feels to be clean!

Father, I know there are areas of my life that are not clean. Help me to see them, and give me a willingness to let you do your cleansing work. "Create in me a pure heart, O God, and renew a steadfast spirit within me" (Ps. 51:10).

Gail Wenos

Do You Pray like You Pack?

He spent the whole night in prayer to God. Luke 6:12 NASB

As a man packeth his suitcase, so is he. My wife packs hers a week before a trip. Not me. I'm the last minute type—throwing stuff in as I'm running out the door, having just enough time to make it to the airport, and begging all the way, "Please, oh, please, Lord, don't let me have a flat tire!"

The entire neighborhood knows when I'm leaving on a trip . . .

"Where is the strap for my carry-on bag?!"

"Who stole my shampoo?!"

"Which one of you girls took my razor, and where are the batteries to my Walkman? Brandon!" I can hear him lock his door so he won't have to give them up.

Holly yells, "Hurry up or you'll miss your flight!"

I love it on the edge. It's me. Unfortunately, it's also the way I pray. It's last minute and in a hurry. After all, I'm the important speaker and author. Sometimes I'm *too* important writing about God to spend time with him. I'm *too* busy leading teens to a life with him to make time to be with him myself.

Then I read *Too Busy Not to Pray* by Bill Hybels. It described me, the man too busy to seek God except when I need him. Without him the day is wasted. A chance to hold his hand is lost forever.

I used to be late for everything. It was my trademark until the Holy Spirit showed me that it was no more than selfishness—me concentrating on me. My prayer life was no different.

 Oh, Lord, my time with you is better than any other time of the day. Instead of waiting for tomorrow, I choose not to leave you at all.

Bill Sanders

Doing Good Work

God saw all that he had made, and it was very good. Genesis 1:31

Our God is a creator. He takes pleasure in creation. In the beginning, he looked at all his hands had done and pronounced it good. When we reflect on our work at the end of the day, do we experience a sense of gratification? Can we, too, say it is good?

How we evaluate our work is important. As a professional speaker, I've learned that some audiences will like me almost regardless of how well I speak. I call that a good audience. They're nice people who respond in an enthusiastic way. But getting an audience like that is not a function of my efforts.

Other audiences are tougher. No matter how hard I work or how well I do, their response is less than enthusiastic. The work is good, but the audience is unappreciative.

The most important question for me is, "Did I do a good job?" Eternally more important than pleasing my audience is pleasing God. It is nice when others are appreciative, but my gratification should come from the creation not from the response.

I believe God wants us to do good work, at home or on the road. He wants us to enjoy the same kind of gratification he experiences. Too often we evaluate our work using the world's standards rather than God's.

 Lord, I want to do good work. Help me to infuse everything I do with a commitment to do the best I am capable of doing, and may my work always honor you.

Mark Sanborn

Easier on the Road

As the deer pants for the water brooks, So my soul pants for Thee, O God. Psalm 42:1 NASB

Have you ever noticed that it's easier to find time for certain things when you're traveling than when you're at home? Reading, writing letters, setting goals, and spending quiet time with God are all a breeze when I'm away from home. But with the remote control in hand, kids fighting, phones ringing, and appointments to make, I carve out time for everyone except God.

Traveling from one speaking engagement to another, always being positive, and having open ears and lengthy counsel for each and every distressing story told was always hard. I would call home complaining. Some of my friends and even my wife felt sorry for me . . . until we had twins!

But now I've grown to love the road. I'm asleep on the plane before takeoff and can have a good drool dripping from my mouth before reaching twenty thousand feet. The last quiet nap I had at home was when I was in the fourth grade! As an added benefit, I don't have to cut anyone's meat, and if two people are arguing in the next row, I don't have to stop it.

Sure I long for and miss my family, but as a road warrior, I get to spend time with God. An hour Bible study is easy in my hotel room. It's just as easy to miss my quiet time ten mornings in a row at home.

God doesn't want his children to come to him just when they are scared or cling to him only when they are in trouble. He longs for them to want to spend time with him even when things are going well.

 Dear Lord, oh that I would thirst for you more than life itself.

Bill Sanders

ET Phone Home

Come to me, all you who are weary and burdened, and I will give you rest. Matthew 11:28

God is always with you to support and encourage you. What a welcome message for a Christian road warrior away from home. But why don't we take him up on his offer? For men, maybe it's our programming: "I am a rock! I'll take care of it myself!" For women, maybe it's come with competing in the male-dominated world of road warriors. For both men and women, it may have something to do with the pride we take in our self-sufficiency. We take our luggage with wheels, our portable notebook computers, our calendar time systems, and our color-coordinated wardrobes that smash neatly into any plane's overhead compartment. We wield our tools of the trade—a Swiss army knife, a folding iron, a sewing kit, earplugs, even balloons to entertain crying babies. We're traveling survivalists—in control and proud of it!

But God has a hard time finding his place in all our survival gear. And many times the stuff is not enough. We feel lonely, disconnected. Like the alien from *ET* who was left alone in a strange world, we try to get by and connect with strangers. But after a time, we miss the hugs of our partners and the play with our children and friends. Just as ET labored frantically to send his message, "ET phone home," we send a similar message. We all want to be home, but thankfully Jesus has provided the phone and the receptionist to reach our true home with God no matter where we travel.

Lord, help me step out of the race to experience your calming presence, your unburdening love, and your centering power. I am phoning home! Thank you for always being there to answer.

Terry Paulson

Far from Blameless

Oh, that my ways were steadfast in obeying your decrees! Then I would not be put to shame when I consider all your commands. Psalm 119:5–6

I was surprised when I read these verses. To understand why, you need to read verses 1–4: "Blessed are they whose ways are blameless, who walk according to the law of the LORD. Blessed are they who keep his statutes and seek him with all their heart. They do nothing wrong; they walk in his ways. You have laid down precepts that are to be fully obeyed."

After reading those verses, I was feeling pretty low. They seemed to have been written by some saintly, holier-than-thou psalmist. Despite my best efforts, my ways most days are far from blameless.

But then I got to verses 5 and 6. Here's the surprise: The psalmist was saying (my paraphrase), "I sure wish I were that way! Then I wouldn't feel so bad about how often I disappoint God."

Hey, he's just like me! And he still made it into the Bible! The psalmist was discouraged. He knew he often fell short of God's high standards.

God is a holy God, but at the same time he is a patient and forgiving God. Christ was the only blameless person ever to live. When we sin, that is the time to look to our Father for forgiveness and be amazed at the chance to try again.

Dear Lord, I want to be blameless before you, but I know only the blood of Jesus makes me that way. Thank you that Jesus died for my sins, past and present. And when I fail, remind me that you are a patient and forgiving God. Then help me to do better in my efforts to please you.

Mark Sanborn

The Faster I Go, the More Behind I Get

You will keep him in perfect peace, Whose mind is stayed on You!
Isaiah 26:3 NKJV

Being on the road can mean backlog at the office. Phone messages, mail, and projects keep piling up. Suddenly, the backlog of unfinished work becomes overwhelming. There simply aren't enough hours in the day to get it all done. Even if there were, my energy seems drained. I reach a point of wanting to chuck the whole mess.

Surely God never intended for our lives to become so stressful. And yet, stress and worry seem to have become a way of life.

Luke 5:16 tells us that when Jesus was mobbed by the demanding crowds, he "often withdrew to lonely places and prayed." Those times of quiet with his Father were times of renewal, giving him strength to continue his ministry.

And that's what our heavenly Father is asking of us—to draw away from the hectic demands of our lives and to rest in his quiet strength. If we would just do that, we'd probably hear him say, "Be still my child. Quit trying to do so much on your own strength. Don't you know that I give strength for the day . . . just take the time to gather it."

Father, there are so many demands on my time and energy. I can't seem to get everything done! The harder I try, the less time I seem to spend with you, my source of strength. Help me to rearrange my priorities, putting my time spent with you first, trusting that you will multiply both my time and energy.

Gail Wenos

Fear No Evil

Yea, though I walk through the valley of the shadow of death, I will fear no evil. Psalm 23:4 KJV

As the plane taxied out to the runway for takeoff, I went through my normal procedure of praying for the trip and the safety of all on board. Immediately after saying amen I heard a strange grinding noise coming from the right side of the plane. I was somewhat unsettled.

The plane stopped. No noise. After a few moments we slowly began to move toward the runway. Once again as the brakes were applied, the same sound increased my uneasiness. Was I imagining this? I reminded myself that this was not the twilight zone and God was on my side.

Before my finger could reach the call button, the silence was broken by an announcement from the cockpit. "This is your captain speaking. Folks, it appears we may have some mechanical problems with one of our landing gears. Too many little lights are going on up here. Your safety is our primary concern. Please be patient as we figure out our next plan of action. Thank you."

I breathed a sigh of relief and said "thank you, thank you, thank you" to my wonderful heavenly Father. Then I settled back in my seat for plan B to be initiated. Over the next few hours as we slowly proceeded through the deplaning process, I had time to reflect on some biblical records. Over and over God reminds us, "Fear not, I am with you."

Heavenly Father, even though I may walk or fly through the valley of the shadow of death, I need not fear. Thanks for reminding me of how you take care of me and protect me on all my travels.

George Hendley

Fear Not

Being in anguish, he prayed more earnestly, and his sweat was like drops of blood falling to the ground. When he rose from prayer and went back to the disciples, he found them asleep, exhausted from sorrow. "Why are you sleeping?" he asked them. "Get up and pray so that you will not fall into temptation." Luke 22:44–46

I said a quick prayer for a skilled mechanic and a short delay. As I waited for the plane to be repaired, my eyes focused on the TV placed in the waiting area to distract the savage beasts angry over their missed connections. Would today's *Headline News* be any different? Would the reporter offer solutions or just report a fresh crop of murders, mayhem, and anniversaries of old disasters? I thought of how easily we, like the disciples on the Mount of Olives, can be lulled into a sorrowful sleep by the drone of negative news and worry over problems yet to be solved. Would Christ have even wasted his time watching? Would he have written letters to Washington demanding new programs? I fear not. On the day before he faced the cross, Jesus knelt in the Garden of Gethsemane and sought guidance in earnest prayer: "Father, if you are willing, take this cup from me; yet, not my will, but yours be done" (Luke 22:42). There was no plea for his disciples to take up their swords in his defense, no plan of escape, just earnest prayer and a trust in God's plan. May we, like Jesus, stay alert so we can see God's opportunities in the midst of obstacles. May we pray earnestly and live boldly trusting in him.

Lord, help me to rise from my preoccupation with problems and my fear of the future to trust your will no matter what life hands me today. Steer my self-sufficient striving into a new dependence on you.

Terry Paulson

37

The Fight

I have fought the good fight, I have finished the race, I have kept the faith. 2 Timothy 4:7

In the verse you just read, notice that Paul doesn't proclaim, "I won!" Today, the preoccupation is with winning. You rarely hear a motivational speaker say, "I tried hard, I didn't give up, and I . . . finished." Yet, for Paul, the victory came in finishing not winning the race.

Sometimes winning the race tempts runners to take shortcuts. Or maybe they overtrain. Perhaps they become more concerned with the outcome than the process. There are many pitfalls for the runner whose obsession is only with winning.

Paul's focus was on how he ran the race. He wasn't running by the world's standards; he was running by God's standards. The victory was in keeping the faith, never compromising, and persistently moving toward the goal of eternity with God. Paul finished the race because he kept running; he had the stamina to persevere. He knew how he ran the race was as important as finishing.

Just as with Paul, how we do what we do is important. Traveling requires stamina. Sometimes I am so tired from traveling I don't have the energy to sleep. And in those moments of weariness, I am discouraged. What does God require at those times? Not that I cross the finish line first, but simply that I keep running the race, that I keep the faith.

Are you fighting the good fight? Or does your stamina waver when you are on the road? The race lasts as long as we live, and the finish line is heaven. Press on until you win the reward that awaits those who finish.

Lord, help me to put one foot in front of the other when I am tired. Life can be a struggle. Give me strength to fight the good fight, and increase my faith as I look toward the finish line of eternity.

Mark Sanborn

Finding Peace in the Midst of Anxiety

Be anxious for nothing, but in everything by prayer and supplication with thanksgiving let your requests be made known to God. And the peace of God, which surpasses all comprehension, shall guard your hearts and your minds in Christ Jesus. Philippians 4:6–7 NASB

It was my oldest daughter, Monica, on the phone. "Mom, I know you're only home for a few days, but I was wondering if you could baby-sit Thursday morning. The kids really miss seeing you."

The kids are Toby, Tim, and Brooke. My three grandchildren live a few short miles from me, yet I only see them a couple times a month. Monica wishes I saw them more often, and I wrestle with regular bouts of guilt. It seems that my work is a calling, given to me as God's work. Yet I am a wife, a mother, a grandmother, and the daughter of a very precious ninety-year-old mother who would also like to see much more of me. How do I know what the Lord's priorities are for me in regard to my responsibilities and important love relationships?

Then when I am home there is, of course, the mail, client calls, the laundry, the dry cleaning, the e-mail, the voice mail, the answering machine, in addition to family and friends. And what about quiet time in your presence, Lord?

Peace only returns when I remember that in and of myself I have no wisdom. God's wisdom for daily direction is my only hope. He alone can show me how to balance life's priorities.

Lord, I confess my confusion. You know my heart; I long to serve you in whatever place you would have me. Please help me rest in the knowledge that you will lead me in the paths of your choice, day by day.

Glenna Salsbury

First Class Service

Serve wholeheartedly, as if you were serving the Lord, not men.
Ephesians 6:7

Once you've flown first class, flying coach is never the same. You *know* there is a difference. You *know* the rolls being served in first class are not the same "hockey pucks" being served in coach. You *know* that once the beverage cart passes, it will disappear forever.

And as your fork is jammed down your throat by the suddenly reclined seat ahead of you or by the elbow of the person next to you, thoughts of first class begin to taunt you.

In first class, you are a name . . . in coach, a number. You realize that even though the destination for both first class and coach are the same, there is a definite difference in the service. And so it is with life.

If we believe we are called to be God's servants here on earth, we need to look at the "service" we offer. Is it first class or coach? When we interact with fellow passengers, check in at the hotel, give our orders to waitresses, meet with clients, or greet the hotel maid, does our demeanor change with the "importance" of the person? Do we categorize them as first class or coach?

I like adding emphasis to the words of Jesus in Matthew 7:12: "In *everything*, do to others what you would have them do to you." He was simply asking us to give nothing but first class service.

Father, keep me mindful of my words, attitudes, and actions. May all that I do today be done with a first class quality. May all your children I meet today receive my best.

Gail Wenos

Gate 34, Gate 32, or the Narrow Gate?

Enter by the narrow gate; for the gate is wide, and the way is broad that leads to destruction, and many are those who enter by it. For the gate is small, and the way is narrow that leads to life, and few are those who find it. Matthew 7:13–14 NASB

Little Rock, Arkansas, Madrid—the flight attendant's voice drones on and on. My mind muses over the amazing realization that one gate leads to Little Rock and the other goes all the way to Madrid. Then, quickly, a thought penetrates this musing: "If you don't know where you are going, any gate will do!"

Where are you going? Are you heading for success or failure? Are you seeking status, pursuing power, fascinated by fame, or mesmerized by money? A Scripture verse echoes in my mind: "What does it profit a man to gain the whole world, and forfeit his soul?" (Mark 8:36 NASB). I realize again that the only destination that really counts is the final destination, which is eternity with or without the Lord—heaven or hell.

Not just any gate will do—I only want the one marked by Christ's love, the gate marked eternity. I raced toward my correct earthly gate, desiring to fulfill obligations, plans, and earthly goals. I wouldn't even consider rushing into the gate that is next to the one I need. I smile and realize the parallel. Spiritually I know which gate is the right gate. It is narrow. It is small. Few find it. But it leads to where I want to go: life everlasting with my Father in heaven.

Father, the wide gate is thronged with people. It leads to destruction. Thank you for leading me to the narrow gate. Help me to lead those I meet to that gate— the one that leads to life eternal.

Naomi Rhode

Get Out That Road Map!

First seek the counsel of the LORD. 1 Kings 22:5

Because of my dyslexia, processing directions is a challenge. I tend to get lost . . . frequently!

Rarely do I rent cars, but on one particular trip I did. Needing to catch a plane at the Columbia, South Carolina, airport, I asked for directions. It didn't take me long to get lost. After stopping for new directions, I took off and eventually hit a dead end. Once more, in a panic, I asked for directions.

It took several more inquiries before I finally made it. Each person seemed to have a different way of getting there . . . unfortunately none of them got *me* there! But the last person made a difference. He said, "What you need is a road map." Taking out his road map, he showed me the way.

Waiting at the airport, I thought, "Lord, You have given me a road map for my life. 'Your word is a lamp to my feet and a light for my path' (Ps. 119:105). But how many times do I try to make decisions based on the advice of others without first consulting you? How many contracts or proposals are signed and accepted without so much as a prayer . . . without checking to see if they fit in with your principles? How many times do I 'lose my way' because I have taken directions from the wrong source?"

Father, you are always ready to give me the direction that I need, and yet there are times when I first seek the counsel of others. Today, as I face decisions, guide me with your Word and show me your principles. Thank you that you do know the way in which I should go.

Gail Wenos

Getting a Bigger Picture

Blessed are the poor in spirit, for theirs is the kingdom of heaven.
Blessed are the meek, for they will inherit the earth. Matthew 5:3, 5

My adrenaline always flows more quickly when an airplane lifts off for an international destination. This particular trip was to Germany. The conferences would each have well over one thousand participants. I was excited because I knew they would be an enthusiastic bunch!

The warmth and incredible hospitality began at the Frankfurt airport. Handmade signs in my favorite color welcomed me. We drove to a rustic lodge nestled on a ridge fed with clean mountain air. People began arriving, and soon the huge lobby was filled with Dutch, German, French, Russian, Czech, Ukrainian, and Swiss participants.

In the driveway outside the revolving doors, I suddenly noticed five people looking up at the hotel, holding on to one another, and crying openly. I touched the arm of my host and asked what was wrong.

"They are East Germans who have never seen a hotel. They are overwhelmed at the thought of being here and are afraid to come in because they feel unworthy. I have spoken with them, and they are waiting outside until their emotions subside a bit."

Lord, have I been rejoicing in my freedom in you? Is your humble spirit evident in my life? Lord Jesus, help me see afresh the multitude of blessings you have given me. Thank you for the freedom to travel at will, to serve you, and to speak of you without fear of reprisal. May I never take any of these gifts for granted.

Glenna Salsbury

The God of All Circumstances

The jailor . . . fell trembling before Paul and Silas. . . . "Sirs, what must I do to be saved?" They replied, "Believe in the Lord Jesus, and you will be saved—you and your household." Then they spoke the word of the Lord to him. Acts 16:29–32

The woman who booked me for the customer service seminar was the director of hospital products. She had been a bottom-line communicator in our telephone conversations prior to the conference. Her national customer base would be in attendance, and she knew what she wanted for them. Knowing these realities did not prepare me for the events that followed.

My presentation covered the key elements of "unsurpassed customer service," and the group seemed especially responsive to my presentation. The applause subsided and the director stepped up next to me and said, "Meet me in the coffee shop at 7:00 A.M. tomorrow morning." Worry launched an immediate attack on my mind.

The waitress had not yet poured our coffee when the director leaned across the breakfast table, looked me right in the eye, and asked, "What do I have to do to be saved?"

I nearly dropped my coffee mug! Softly I responded, "You simply ask Jesus Christ to make himself real to you." Then I began to give a brief explanation of sin, the cross, and the resurrection.

She responded quietly, "My secretary is a Christian. She's been praying for me for five years. I was too embarrassed to let her know that I didn't know what to do to really become a Christian."

Oh, Lord, how I praise you for your sovereign hand. You send us into the places you want us to be. You prepare the circumstances and the hearts.

Glenna Salsbury

Going Home

As you look forward to the day of God and speed its coming.
2 Peter 3:12

I t sure feels good going home." No truer words could be said for the business traveler. Heading home. Volumes have been written about people longing for their homes and loved ones in faraway lands.

I am no different. When I am finished with my last talk, I start focusing on the five most important people in the world to me—my wife, my three kids, and my mother. Nothing else captures my attention. I wonder what they are eating and doing, who will greet me, and if they miss me or if they're too busy. I long to see, hug, and kiss them.

God longs for us in the same way. All day, every day, he wonders why we don't have time for him, when we will love him enough to tell someone of him, when we will need him enough to want to be with him all day long.

I would be heartbroken if I returned home only to find my wife and kids playing a game and not bothering to acknowledge my presence. Can you imagine how empty you would feel?

You are made in God's image. He hurts also. He loves you and deeply wants you to love him. He has countless blessings if you will only look to him to meet your needs and realize that everything good comes from him. This isn't our final home. Heaven is. We aren't in a place full of life headed to a place of death. It's the other way around. Eternal life awaits us!

 Dear Father, I'm forever with you. What could be better? And knowing you are waiting, I'll be home soon.

Bill Sanders

The Good in All Things

And we know that in all things God works for the good of those who
love him, who have been called according to his purpose. Romans 8:28

This verse blows my mind! A canceled flight, for my own good? Ridiculous! A missed meeting or lost account to my benefit? Give me a break!

The problem, at least in part, is that we make God too small and too big at the same time. He's "too big" to be concerned with the details of our life; after all, he's got a lot more pressing issues to deal with than our missed connection. But that's where we make him "too small." We can't really fathom a God who deals with world hunger and missed connections simultaneously. Neither can we understand how he could orchestrate an infinitely complex and interconnected world in which our missed flight will benefit us somehow and still make sense for the other people affected.

Lacking faith, our focus is on the immediate rather than the eternal. We can see the immediate inconvenience or frustration, but it is difficult to imagine what character-building, eternal consequences God has in mind.

I can only hope that through practice and God's grace, my mind will comprehend the significance of Romans 8:28. And then maybe I will have grasped the essence of faith.

 Father, increase my faith. Help me to be secure in your promise that all things—everything!—works together for my good. Remind me that you are more interested in my eternal welfare than my immediate gratification. Show me that in the minor inconveniences and the major traumas of life, your hand sustains.

Mark Sanborn

Good News from Afar

As cold waters to a thirsty soul, so is good news from a far country.
Proverbs 25:25 KJV

Traveling can be fun. It can also be very tiring. It's just one of the challenges that goes with being a road warrior. Staying in touch with those left behind is one of the most important aspects for keeping yourself refreshed while on the road.

Carrying a photo or two with you puts that favorite face or faces in clear view from time to time. Yet there's nothing quite like the sound of a familiar voice on the telephone.

The people back home need to know you're thinking of them. When you're excited and have good news, they want you to share it with them. But even when you're tired or lonely, they want to hear from you. They also want to share with you the news that can bring a smile to your face. "You got the job with company X, and they want to expand on the contract." That makes your day!

A well timed and thoughtfully planned phone call is rejuvenating. It can be mentally and physically refreshing to hear good news whether you're the one on the road or at home. "Did Johnny do well on his report card? Has the new furniture arrived yet? Are you feeling better today? I miss you too. We'll spend time together this weekend. I promise." When you call in or they call you, be ready to drink in *and* pour out good news and enjoy the refreshment it brings.

 Heavenly Father, remind me to share the good news with those on the home front. Show me how I can share my best not only with my clients but also with my family and staff back home.

George Hendley

The Greatest of These

And now these three remain: faith, hope and love. But the greatest of
these is love. 1 Corinthians 13:13

Years ago, a popular song said, "What the world needs now is love, sweet love. That's the only thing that there's just too little of." The love the song was referring to was the kind of brotherly love developed between friends. That love is okay, but the love that a spiritual road warrior needs to share to make a real difference in the world is God's love.

The love that distinguishes you from just another traveler is the love that has heart, commitment, integrity, courage, kindness, and compassion. God's love is the badge of Christianity. When you walk in love and talk in love, people will notice. You become so pleasantly unusual that others take a second look at what you do and give a second listen to what you say. Try loving the unappreciated ticket agent at the airport or the busy flight attendant on a crowded airplane and notice the difference in what comes back to you. People are to be loved with God's love.

What is it that makes you stand out from the crowd? It's the love you live and the love you share. Remember, God's love never fails. It's what the world really needs and what there's just too little of.

Almighty God, you are love and the author of love. Teach me to love others as you love me—unconditionally. Give me the opportunities to practice your love on a daily basis, not just with those I know but also with complete strangers.

George Hendley

Holding Forth the Word of Life

Holding forth the word of life; that I may rejoice in the day of Christ, that I have not run in vain, neither laboured in vain. Philippians 2:16 KJV

I was finishing up the last training session in a three-day trip. In the final minutes of the training session, I saw an opportunity to share a verse from Proverbs that fit well with the material. As I finished quoting the verse, a lady near the front of the room smiled at me.

As the participants were leaving, this same smiling lady came to me and said, "I knew you were a Christian by the way you spoke. I could see the light in your eyes. But when you quoted that verse, you reminded me of a minister." She thanked me for being bold enough to share a verse from Scripture. It didn't dawn on me that it took boldness to speak a truth, yet in reviewing the situation, I could understand her comment.

The world is a difficult place for a Christian to speak up and speak out. It's not always politically correct to openly voice your beliefs, especially if others are vocal and adamant against your standards. Thank God we live in a country that values freedom of speech.

When we speak words of life, we can rest assured that someone is going to appreciate our candor. Are you looking for the opportunities to shine or shying away from the opportunities to share? God needs us to use our talents and abilities as his ambassadors wherever we go.

God, show me those opportunities to hold forth your Word. Teach me to be wise and bold when it comes to sharing your message with others.

George Hendley

Honors Bestowed—the Journey Rewarded

And you will be called by a new name, Which the mouth of the LORD will designate. You will also be a crown of beauty in the hand of the LORD, And a royal diadem in the hand of your God. Isaiah 62:2–3 NASB

We are travelers in life—passionately pursuing goals we feel will glorify God. Do you ever wonder if the journey will be rewarded, if honors will be bestowed?

After speaking for over twenty years and being involved in my chosen profession, an "earthly honor" was bestowed on me: My journey was rewarded with a "new name" and a new responsibility as president of the National Speakers Association. It has been a journey rewarded with a family of friends and colleagues I love. It is also a pleasant title to remember the rest of my life.

For all of us, such rewards are wonderful. However, when I reflect on Isaiah 62:2, one of the verses I have chosen this year to meditate on regularly, I smile. How our earthly titles pale in light of God's grand promises! I am called by a "new name." I am a crown of beauty in the Lord's hand, a royal diadem in God's hand.

Is it wonderful to have the privilege of position and responsibility with my peers? Yes! But it is inconceivably joyous to be given a new name and delight from my Lord as a child of God! We are blessed when we acknowledge his honor as our journey's best reward.

 Father, you chose me and I respond with humility and joy at your calling and your reward. May I live in the power of my new name.

Naomi Rhode

If This Is Tuesday, I Must Be in Cleveland

Peace I leave with you; my peace I give you. I do not give to you as the world gives. Do not let your hearts be troubled and do not be afraid.
John 14:27

Crack! Zap! Thunder and lightning perform pyrotechnics behind the half-closed drapes. I awake—startled, a little afraid, and confused. Where am I? It doesn't rain like this in California. Why is this sheet so scratchy? Where's my husband? Ah, now I remember.

Crack! Zap! Where are you, Lord? It's frightening to be suddenly roused and not know where I am. My heart is still pounding, but if I breathe very deliberately and center my thoughts on you, I know I'm not alone. This is the hard part of the work I feel you've called me to do—being alone at night in a strange bed and a strange town on the night before I present an opening keynote address to another group of strangers.

I'd sure feel better if I thought there were times when your disciples wanted to stay home. Surely Peter wanted some home-cooked food, the warmth of his family, and his comfortable, albeit rustic, surroundings. Surely he complained just a little bit? Was he not scared at times too? Did he ever have to slow down his breathing and remember all the different times you said you'd always be with him?

 Dear God, I hope so. And somehow, in my heart, I know your disciples were just like me. Thanks for letting me know that I don't need to be afraid. Thanks for being with me in a strange place.

Eileen McDargh

The Importance of Looking Up

Then Jesus entered a house, and again a crowd gathered, so that he and his disciples were not even able to eat. Mark 3:20

Maybe you've found that the best policy on airplanes is "Don't look up!" By establishing eye contact, you might attract the interest of the grandmother next to you who is prepared to tell you all about her grandchildren for the next three hours. Or you could get an earful from a fellow traveler about how bad the airlines are. Then how would you get any work or reading done?

I've employed the "Don't look up!" strategy for thousands of air miles. There have been times when I was so physically and emotionally drained that I needed the time to myself. But often it was an avoidance technique.

I think there are times when God wants me to look up—to politely listen (at least for awhile) to the grandchildren stories, or to allow someone to vent his or her frustration.

Sometimes my ministry is no farther away than the hurting soul in the seat next to me.

There were many times when Jesus needed to be alone for prayer and rejuvenation. But when he was with people, he was really with them. Sometimes the throngs were so overwhelming he couldn't even eat. He was too busy healing, teaching, encouraging, counseling, helping, and listening. Wherever he saw people, he saw a chance to minister.

In your travels, make it a habit to look up. The opportunity to minister might be coming down the aisle pushing a drink cart.

Lord, sometimes it is easier not to look up. Help me to avoid shutting out the people around me. Let me see my travels as an opportunity to serve you through serving them.

Mark Sanborn

In Search of True Riches

Do not wear yourself out to get rich; have the wisdom to show restraint. Cast but a glance at riches, and they are gone, for they will surely sprout wings and fly off to the sky like an eagle. Proverbs 23:4–5

Get on that plane! Make that sale! Give that speech! Keep that career moving! I enjoy working hard. And isn't getting ahead using my God-given gifts what it's all about?

I once counseled a man in a hospice who was dying of liver cancer. In a private conversation he said, with tears streaming down his face, "I spent fifty-two years of my life preparing to live, and now I have no time. What are you going to say that will make any difference?" I listened to his despair and helped him talk about preparing his family and exploring his own faith. I hope what I had to say helped him; little did he know how much his words have helped me. That conversation is never far away as I race through life's never ending stream of urgencies.

Whether it's through earthquakes in L.A., floods in the Midwest, or hurricanes in Florida, riches can seemingly sprout wings. I've often thought, "What would a successful road warrior like me want on his tombstone?" "He finished everything on his to do list." "Here lies the man who died with the most unused frequent flyer miles in history."

From the shadow of the cross, Jesus calls us out of the rat race of earthly priorities into a relationship of faith and service.

Lord, help me to claim your victory and rest in the sufficiency of your grace every day. Keep me centered on the true riches of faith. Keep me serving not just striving.

Terry Paulson

53

Insight from an In-flight Magazine

If anyone would come after me, he must deny himself and take up his cross and follow me. For whoever wants to save his life will lose it, but whoever loses his life for me and for the gospel will save it.
Mark 8:34–35

The in-flight magazine contained a simple statement, a reason for heart attacks: "People prone to heart attacks dwell on themselves and find stress and anxiety during their self-indulgent concentration."

Lord, that's me! In amazement, I realized I hadn't given heed to others all day. I had been so into myself and my needs that I hadn't thought much about the needs of others.

It wasn't the ticket agent's fault the computer was down, but all I wanted was my seat assignment. That fellow traveler just wanted to share a cup of coffee and a chat while all I wanted was to be left alone. There was that grumpy looking bell clerk who deserved and probably needed more from me than a curt thank you. Too much of what I did today was only what I wanted and needed. What did they call it? "Self-indulgent concentration."

Dear Lord, please don't let me become so self-absorbed, like the runner who never sees anything but red clay and the same blur on the sideline. Get me out of my narrow needs and onto your way. Thank you for the opportunity to try again tomorrow to let your Spirit lead me.

Eileen McDargh

Integrity on the Road

May the words of my mouth and the meditations of my heart be pleasing in your sight, O LORD, my Rock and my Redeemer. Psalm 19:14

This popular yet seldom memorized or acted out verse is the key to staying pure while on the road, where temptations seem to multiply. This verse has been a friend of mine for quite some time, and when I remember it, it helps me live in a way that would make my family and God proud.

The words of my mouth. I love to speak what's on my mind! It gets me in trouble. Words hurt and cut and deliver pain. When I don't attempt to live out this verse, my mouth delivers destruction, but when I do, I build up people and God.

Meditations. I get them from what I see and hear. If I control what goes into my mind through my ears and eyes, I seldom have to be ashamed of what is floating around in my heart.

God's sight. He sees everything. There is no such thing as a secret sin. Why do I always act like mere clay and try to fool myself?

Oh, my loving Lord! Yes, you are my Lord. You are my everything and far more important than anything. I stand on your Word and your promises. My life's desire is to be pleasing in your sight. I hate it when I make you cry and my enemy laugh. You have rebuilt my heart and life and given me nothing but forgiveness, love, and peace.

Lord, I'm so sorry when I try to sin in my dark places and speak before I think of what you would have me say. Help me to be pure and full of integrity.

Bill Sanders

It Won't Matter Then

I consider that our present sufferings are not worth comparing with the glory that will be revealed in us. Romans 8:18

I was introduced to the joys of travel as a child. Every summer our family took car trips. We didn't have lots of money, so we stayed in clean but inexpensive hotels. More often than not, we ate picnic lunches my mother had packed away in the ice chest in the trunk of the car. It was a different kind of travel from the business travel I do today but better because I was doing it with my family. My dad worked hard all year so we could afford those family vacations.

My father passed away on a cold and dreary November day after a valiant struggle with cancer. He was a committed Christian, and he was an inspiration for many in the final months of his life as his faith deepened and he faced death without fear.

He was only sixty-two years old when he died. Just weeks before his death, my mother told him that when he got to heaven, she wanted him to ask God why he took him from his earthly home so early.

My dad was a thoughtful man of few words. He put it all in perspective when he smiled and said, "When I get to heaven, it won't even matter."

Father, help me to remember that all our pleasures and joys as well as our pain and suffering will fade away completely when we finally travel home to be with you. Remind me that so much of what worries me and occupies my thoughts today won't really matter when I meet you face to face.

Mark Sanborn

I've Got More Ribbons than You!

My little children, let us not love in word, neither in tongue; but in deed and in truth. 1 John 3:18 KJV

Remember Christ and the many crowds that followed him? His disciples were always trying to keep people away from him. After all, he didn't have time. But Christ was there for anyone who needed him, anyone who reached out, anyone who had a question or just wanted to talk. And he was the Master Spiritual Road Warrior.

A few years ago, I sat next to a prominent professional at a luncheon during a convention. He was noticeably unimpressed with his luncheon companions, and after a few attempts at conversation, I gave up. Shortly, a more prominent and highly respected person came by and spoke to him and then engaged me in conversation, being quite complimentary. It was amazing how talkative my luncheon neighbor became after he realized that I was accepted by the "elite."

No sooner did I start to judge him when a little voice inside my head said, "You are no different than him!" What?! I was reminded of the many times I had lost an opportunity to love someone because I was caught up in wanting to be with the "popular" group and had no time for the unknown. Now I try to remember that the obnoxious, boring, or unknown person who is monopolizing my time at any given function may be the one who needs to see the love of God in action. Hopefully, they will.

Lord, thank you for loving me. Remind me always how special each person is in your eyes. Give me the heart to love them all, not with words but with action.

Lori White

The Joy of Litter

I found a high school near the hotel today and decided to run on the track rather than exercise in the stuffy, small room the hotel calls a gym. The crisp fall air made the run that much more invigorating, and there was much to occupy my mind.

The track was littered with last night's high school homecoming exultations: banners, confetti, streamers, even the remnants of a papier-mâché horse that had pulled a homecoming float.

The teenagers were slowly heading onto the field for cleanup duty as I wound my way around the last lap and felt my face break into a broad smile as memories of my past flooded my mind.

58

I wonder if they would think that the "old lady" running on their track once shared a field like this one . . . and built blessed memories that would last a lifetime. Maybe it was time to do a little joyful littering of my own to mark my new age!

Thank you, Lord, for that spirit of human joy that lets us break the traditional role of neat and clean to throw expressions of excitement into the air. As long as we clean up our happiness, Lord, what more is there left to say but thank you?

Eileen McDargh

Keep Swimming

Now all has been heard; here is the conclusion of the matter: Fear God
and keep his commandments, for this is the whole duty of man.
Ecclesiastes 12:13

Airport shops sell the silliest things. In Fort Lauderdale I saw the amazing—he actually swims!—battery operated scuba diver. What really got my attention was that Mr. Diver was swimming in a fishbowl only several inches larger in diameter than the length of his body! Stroke and kick and thunk—head first into the side of the bowl.

Do you ever feel like that? The irony of his situation didn't escape me. Sometimes my perseverance is my pitfall. Career: two strokes forward and thunk. Relationships: two strokes forward and thunk. Habits I want to change, goals I want to achieve . . . the same frustration. And with each stroke, the denial of the limitations.

The limitations we face aren't always self-imposed; sometimes they are the result of the bowl of this world in which we swim. Circumstances confine us, but to quit swimming forward seems like giving up.

The writer of Ecclesiastes must have had a fishbowl experience, but on a larger scale. Hedonistic pleasure, riches, recognition, and success brought him to the same conclusion: "It's all two strokes forward and thunk."

So why keep swimming? After examining the futility of finding eternal significance in the fishbowl, Solomon found his purpose in knowing God and keeping his commandments.

Lord, it feels as though I'm in a fishbowl not much bigger than I am. Sometimes it all seems meaningless, despite the success I achieve. Only by knowing you and keeping your commandments can I continue to keep swimming forward—despite the thunks.

Mark Sanborn

A Lamp to My Feet

Your word is a lamp to my feet and a light for my path. Psalm 119:105

Waking up in the middle of the night to a strange sound, when you're in strange room, in a faraway place can be disturbing. It may just be the guy across the hall fumbling with his key and talking to himself. Yet that's enough to get you out of bed to do a quick hall check. But the problem is, where is everything?

When you're at home, the bedside table is just to your right with the phone and the lamp on it. You know your room layout and could maneuver it in your sleep. Therein lies the problem. This is a hotel room. Where is the bedside table, the phone, the lamp?

Slowly, cautiously, I make my way to the bathroom and turn on a light. After quickly checking the hall, I'm back in bed and thinking to myself, "I should be better prepared for situations like this."

Knowing that the world would give us plenty of dark moments in strange places, God provided us with the light that never burns out nor needs replacement: the Bible.

The Gideons provide Bibles for hotel rooms across the country. Because of the Gideons, you can always find a spiritual "night-light," a Bible, in your room. The light and understanding from God's Word quickly dispel the darkness that sometimes clouds the mind.

Heavenly Father, you gave me your Word as a lamp to my feet and a light for my path. Thank you for preparing me for all my adventures.

George Hendley

Lasting Glory

Last night I listened to some music by Geoff Moore and the Distance. Moore wrote one of the songs in a cemetery. It is titled "After All Is Said and Done." The lyrics ask, "What really lasts?" After all is said and done and our earthly bodies are in the ground, for what will we be remembered?

That question eventually perplexes anyone who thinks about the meaning of his or her life, but I ask that question more often and more poignantly when I'm on the road. Sitting on an airplane two thousand miles away from friends and family, I've often thought, "What's the point?"

Paul tells us that the whole point is to know and honor God. Nothing else lasts. Only what we do to serve him is "the glory of that which lasts!" The time, travels, and sacrifice that Paul invested were all to the glory of God and his Son Jesus Christ. Paul wasn't trying to build a reputation, rise to the top of his profession, or make a lot of money. He was simply focusing on what is important "after all is said and done."

The essence of our faith is the assurance that if we live our lives to glorify God, we are building a lasting legacy. It gives point and purpose to the time and sacrifices we make on the road.

61

 Dear Lord, someday all will be said and done. My life on earth will be over. I want my friends and family to be able to know that—first and foremost—I knew you and loved you and served you with all my heart. I want to spend my life investing in what will last.

Mark Sanborn

A Letter to My Son

Fathers, do not exasperate your children; instead, bring them up in the training and instruction of the Lord. Ephesians 6:4

Dear Russell,

I have just returned from a trip on the road and had planned a full day of catch up work—write some letters, organize my office, even get those taxes done early. Then there was an unpleasant call and a lost major contract.

It made me realize that there are more important things in my life. Russell, if I do those things on Saturday, I will miss out on attending a birthday party with you and your mommy. There is going to be a pony there, and you have never seen one before. There is also going to be a parade on Saturday. Neither were very important to me a few days ago, but now I'll lose my day planner on Saturday and will spend that time with you at the parade. You'll never experience a parade for the first time again. The office work and the taxes will wait, and in the big picture of life, those things really won't make much of a difference. But what will make a difference is spending time together. It sure puts a different perspective on what was so worrisome to me yesterday. I'll have lots of blank time in my planner when you're out discovering the world. I'll have so much time I won't know what to do with it. Then I can be productive. Then I can write letters, do my taxes early, and organize the office. Saturday is our day and nothing or no one will take it from us.

 Dear God, help me to keep my priorities in order.

Tim Richardson
(Adapted from *Jump Starts: Words of Wit and Wisdom to Supercharge Your Day,* 1999 by Tim Richardson, edited by J. Lenora King)

62

Letting Go and Letting God

I have learned to be content whatever the circumstances. I know what it is to be in need, and I know what it is to have plenty. I have learned the secret of being content in any and every situation, whether well fed or hungry, whether living in plenty or in want. I can do everything through him who gives me strength. Philippians 4:11–13

I'm sitting in a meeting. I know I'm here because I checked my schedule, yet I feel as though I'm outside looking in. Things are going fast, and no one seems to be in charge. Maybe it's the pizza I ate three days ago that has upset my mental software. Should I interrupt and tell 'em how it ought to be? Should I risk saying something when I'm not even sure I have anything worth saying? Should I stay quiet and let things run their course? No! I have the answer: Let go and let God.

How easy it is to think that we are the center of the universe . . . that the meeting would not succeed without our answers . . . that the weight of the day rests on our actions and our wisdom. We are called to serve and to make a difference, but we rest in the knowledge and faith that it is God who works and lives through us.

Help me, Lord, to let go of my frantic strivings and to rest in your revealing grace. Help me to know in my heart that my real task is service in your name, to rise above the impatient roar of today and follow in your footsteps at your pace.

Bob Sherer

Listening to the Still, Small Voice

And after the earthquake a fire; but the LORD was not in the fire: and after the fire a still small voice. 1 Kings 19:12 KJV

The lounge near gate 4 was crawling with people! Families were returning home from a Thanksgiving weekend. A young family was seated near me, and I overheard the thirtysomething husband speak—very gently—to his wife. "Next year I'd like to go hunting over this vacation time. Would that be okay with you?"

Her response was equally gentle and caring. "Sure, that would be fun for you."

The husband then picked up his blue-eyed boy from the stroller and said, "Let me take Matthew and change his diaper before we board the plane."

I sensed the presence of God's Spirit in these lives. I could hear him in the tone of their voices and the quality of their conversational exchanges.

The flight to San Diego took less than an hour. As we deplaned I caught a glimpse of the young husband in the distance. The Spirit nudged me, "Tell him you see me in him." My mind responded rationally, "That would be embarrassing! What if he isn't a Christian?"

The young man and I were the only two people in the baggage claim area. I smiled at him and said, "Your family reflects the Lord's love and grace."

He looked shocked for a moment and then recovered. "We are so grateful for him in our lives."

Twenty minutes of conversation ensued. Both Tim and I were thoroughly encouraged in the Spirit!

Dearest Holy Spirit, keep me aware of your still, small voice. May I see and hear what you are doing in the world.

Glenna Salsbury

Living Boldly

For the word of God is living and powerful. Hebrews 4:12 NKJV

Travel can be intimidating, even for seasoned pros like you and me. Among strangers and service providers, I've noticed that I tend to be more timid. I move quietly and keep to myself, unless, of course, there is a problem. Then I often become bold, but sometimes for the wrong reasons. My boldness seems more like aggression.

The Bible tells us the Word of God is "living and powerful." If the Word of God is powerful, why do our lives sometimes seem powerless? The problem is a matter of choice: So few Christians, myself included, claim the power that is available to them on a daily basis.

God's power, when we claim it, makes us bold. But rather than making us bold in a way that is brash or self-serving, it gives us a boldness that allows us to move confidently through the challenges that travel and life present. It is a boldness that comes from knowing that ultimately there is no person, power, or event that can ever defeat God's love for us.

Boldness also creates power, and power is the ability to affect change. The power of God in our lives should manifest itself as the ability to affect people in a positive way, to draw them to the Lord not drive them away.

Dear Lord, I claim your power today! Use it first to change my own heart and to make me more like you. Then let your power in my life influence those I come in contact with as I travel.

Mark Sanborn

The Long and Grateful Road

And do not forget to do good and to share with others, for with such sacrifices God is pleased. Hebrews 13:16

I am caught up in the work, the responsibilities, and the traffic in my life and my mind. Presentation after presentation. Face after face. My audiences seem to enjoy what is being said, but does it matter?

After another presentation in what seemed like just another town, I was approached by a woman who took my hand as she spoke. "My son heard you, and his life was changed." I asked the woman where I might have had the pleasure of speaking to her son. She replied, "He was in prison and had been in and out of trouble most of his life." Since then, he has set out to earn a GED for high school completion. He was also paroled and is now working and learning how to live life without alcohol and drugs.

In our professional lives, we are often well paid. But for most of us, it is seldom the treasures we earn that hold the most value. Many of us offer our time, talent, and resources for no monetary gain and end up being blessed beyond what we could ever imagine. For me, I thank God every day for the gift of working with the recovering and still suffering alcoholics and addicts who yearn for God's power, grace, and hope.

Lord, send a soul across my path—a soul who needs a smile, a helping hand, a word of encouragement—and then help me to perform your work. Lord, give me strength today to make a difference in another person's life. Let me share the gifts you have given me, for I can only keep you near by giving you away to others.

Bob Sherer

Love Away from Home

Husbands, love your wives, just as Christ also loved the church and gave Himself up for her. Ephesians 5:25 NASB

The desk clerk fairly beamed when she announced to me: "I have a message for you!" She pulled a piece of a paper from her pocket and showed it to me. "Bill loves you most."

A fellow employee from the back heard our exchange and came running out to see me. "I wanted to know who you were," she exclaimed.

"So, is he going to ask you to marry him?" they both demanded. Obviously such a note could only come from an ardent suitor.

"Well," I replied. "I'd certainly do it again if he asked me. We've been married for thirteen years!" What a smile it brought to me to think of his enduring love.

Oh, how I appreciate my husband and the love he shows over and over again. But how much greater is God's love. Like an ardent suitor, he sends me the blessings of the day. He writes his messages in his Word that convict, encourage, and enliven my day. He comes to me in the silence of prayer as if breathing at my same pace, communicating his love and peace.

Thank you, Lord, for my strong, supportive, loving partner you have planted like grace in my life. Keep our love alive. Bring us back together again and again. May my faith in you, Lord, be ever greater than our enduring love.

Eileen McDargh

Loving Enemies You Meet on the Road

You have heard that it was said, You shall love your neighbor and hate your enemy; But I tell you, Love your enemies and pray for those who persecute you. Matthew 5:43–44 AMP

I once saw a man take out his frustration on a baggage handler. I didn't intervene, but the obnoxious road warrior paid for his outburst. His bags did not go to Chicago; they went to Japan. I laughed, somehow pleased that the jerk had to pay. I tipped well, hoping my bags would get on the right plane! Later, I wondered whether that business traveler was any different from me at my worst on the road. There have been moments on the road I'm not proud of. I'm sure there have been times when my bags could have suffered a similar fate. I wondered if the angry stranger felt remorse after he calmed down. Whatever his regret, I'm sure his anger was rekindled when he arrived in Chicago without bags.

Anger in our world seems to create never ending cycles of hate and revenge. In our walk of faith, Jesus calls us to see difficult people as "extra grace required" challenges. The next time you catch yourself ready to attack an "enemy" you meet on the road, say to yourself: "What an idiot . . . who is created in God's image and I am called to love."

 Lord, give me the strength to love my enemies. Help me to break my own chains of hate and replace them with love. Help me to forgive and pray for those who in any way make my journey more difficult. Help me to work for understanding instead of revenge.

Terry Paulson

Making Time

. . . for it is time to seek the LORD. Hosea 10:12

I don't have the time. . . ." This is a favorite excuse made plausible by the kind of schedule many of us maintain. And the road is a further excuse. It seems necessary to abandon those things that we would never give up at home: Devotions and quality time with loved ones are often the first to go.

I've learned that we seldom have time for what is important in our lives, but we must make the time. Of course we can't literally create hours and minutes, but we can reallocate the time that has been given us for what is important.

What have you given up under the guise of "no time" when you're on the road? Do you have a regular devotional time? My buddy Titus gets up early enough each day to have a cup of coffee and spend some quiet time with God. He calls that time "having coffee with Dad." No quality time with loved ones? Schedule a family phone time each night.

What God desires for us is infinitely better than anything we could desire or attain for ourselves, but we must make the time for God to fill us with those good things.

Lord, today I pray for an honesty that will let me see the excuses I use for not doing what you desire for me on the road. I pray for strength to make the time for those things so I can become the kind of person you desire. Show me how to prioritize my agenda when I travel.

Mark Sanborn

69

Meeting the Messiah Today

I tell you the truth, whatever you did for one of the least of these brothers of mine, you did for me. Matthew 25:40

It's easy to complain about how rude people can be on the road. It's even easier to agonize over the lack of service. But when was the last time you looked at yourself in a mirror and thought about what others see in you?

What if you were approached by a man on a flight who called you by name and said, "I am sorry for bothering you, but I must tell you about my vision. You see, in my vision I saw your face and heard your name, and I was told you will meet the Messiah today. I don't know when or where, but you will meet him." Would such a vision make a difference in how you act? Would you treat those you meet in a more positive way? Would you see your fellow road warrior in the seat next to you in a new light? Would you forgive as the Messiah forgives? Would you encourage as Christ encouraged others he met on the road?

Christ is among us every day and calls us to be transformed by his Spirit. May we in faith take on the aura of love, respect, and service that radiates from him. May the Lord's vibrant light and compelling love show in everything we do. In meeting us may people come to say, "Truly the Messiah has indeed come to all of us!"

Lord, help me never to forget that you are with me every day on every step of my journey. Praise God that when I greet and serve others, I serve you.

Terry Paulson

Of Wine and Witness

For we cannot help speaking about what we have seen and heard.
Acts 4:20

I was sharing a glass of wine with a group of executives who had just attended one of my programs. There was the usual banter, political complaints, and the mandatory jokes. After a joke of questionable taste, I did not laugh. Another executive, who had not seen my response, told the men how glad he was that John, "the uptight Christian," had left! Had Peter and Paul ever felt what I was feeling? If I speak up, they'll think I'm a fanatic too! The words didn't come easy, but they came. "I hope that doesn't mean I have to go to my room. I'm one of those Christians too." The apologies flowed, but I interrupted, "Hey, I'm no saint, just forgiven. Somehow people think you have to be terminally serious and judgmental to be a Christian. God came to give us joy, not to take it away. I'm not comfortable with some jokes, but Jesus wouldn't have been invited to so many parties if he didn't have a sense of humor."

Talking about one's faith certainly was not politically correct for the early apostles. Fresh from their encounter with the risen Lord, however, Peter and John spoke passionately about the gospel to all who would listen. They were commanded by the authorities not to teach in the name of Jesus, but they continued to proclaim the Good News. They couldn't stop talking about it! Knowing the risen Lord, we can do nothing less.

Lord, fuel my passion for my faith and give me the words to bring it to life for those I meet on the road. Use my words and actions to show the joy and the power you alone provide.

Terry Paulson

Oh, the Tongue!

He that keepeth his mouth keepeth his life. Proverbs 13:3 KJV

Traveling can be such a wearisome task. Although it looks glamorous to those who do not travel often, we frequent travelers know that being away from the security and comfort of our families and familiar surroundings can take its toll. Sometimes patience wears thin, tolerance levels falter, and the tongue forgets who is in charge. Things are said without realizing the effect our words have on those who hear.

Once I was on the same flight with a minister who is well known in his denomination. Upon arriving at our destination, we all disembarked and encountered some difficulty securing our luggage. In the process of working things out, this man was very rude to several people. As I watched him, I thought about his position and the impact of his words on people. His words were definitely different now than the times when I had heard him speak from the platform. Sadly, he wasn't even aware of the effect his words were having on those around him.

King Solomon wrote in Proverbs 18:21: "Death and life are in the power of the tongue" (KJV). Regardless of where we are, as Christians we have a responsibility to speak words of life. No matter what circumstances we encounter in our travels, the way to keep our life and to bring life to others is to keep control of our mouths. Otherwise, we fall short of being ambassadors of the one who has called us.

 Dear Lord, thank you for using me to speak to others on your behalf. Be a constant reminder to me that my tongue can build up or tear down and help me always to use words of life that encourage.

Lori White

Okay, Where's the Lesson?

Do not let your hearts be troubled. John 14:1

People often say, when trouble comes, look for the lesson the Lord is sending. Okay, I'm looking for the lesson, but I'd be happier if the Lord hadn't canceled that flight to teach me! Why so many troubles, Lord? Even the countless joys and achievements that mean the most to me have come with their share of troubles.

God doesn't eliminate our troubles, but he does change how we look at them . . . and beyond them. I know that when I try to shove troubles aside, they have an uncanny tendency of rolling right back at me with ever increasing speed. When I commit my past, present, and future troubles to God, however, it's like rolling them away into the empty tomb Jesus left behind. It's nice to know that as a Christian I don't have to break under pressure; I can use my faith to break out of its crippling hold! Trouble knocked again at the door, but hearing faith within, it hurried away. Praise God, and send me my next lesson.

 Lord, to be troubled about the future is to distrust you. To be troubled about the present is to be impatient with you. To be troubled for what is already past is to be angry with you. To believe in you is to rest my troubled heart in your peace. Help me believe.

Terry Paulson

73

On the Road Again—Wearing a Pink Ribbon

There is an appointed time for everything. . . . A time to weep, and a time to laugh; A time to mourn, and a time to dance. Ecclesiastes 3:1, 4 NASB

It's a beautiful fall day. The leaves are brilliant shades of yellow, orange, and red as if signifying the special nature of this trip. I'm wearing a pink ribbon in support of the two and a half million women who currently have breast cancer and another one million who are unaware that they have it.

Statistics mean more when they include someone we know and love, a family we care about, and a soul that has made us laugh.

I met Debra and Gary on the road and came to love them as family. We laughed together, cried together during the dark days of Deb's long struggle with cancer, and recently mourned together over the loss of her life. Now I'm here to celebrate her life and to fight with her family and friends for a cure for this awful disease.

There are many causes to fight for, many different ribbons to wear. It is just one of the privileges we are blessed with as believers—to take the Lord's compassion, love, and concern to the friends we meet in our travels, and to join our voices with those of other concerned people to fight physical diseases and to encourage with the message of Christ's love and compassion. My challenge to you, traveler, is this: Tithe some of your travel time to encourage, cheer, "weep and mourn," as well as "laugh and dance" with people along the road!

Lord, what a privilege it is to encourage the faith of those who fight disease. Be with us as we work together for a healthier world.

Naomi Rhode

On Wings of Eagles

Those who hope in the LORD will renew their strength. They will soar on wings like eagles; they will run and not grow weary, they will walk and not be faint. Isaiah 40:31

Another red-eye flight and just my luck, the baby behind me is an emerging opera singer who never sleeps on planes. I need my strength. Studies say I need 7.9 hours of sleep a night. How do I make myself sleep? Where's the off button for my brain? I'm weary, and I won't be ready for that meeting!" Sound familiar? It does to me. And just when I'm ready to join the baby in crying, the Word of God comes to give me strength. I take refuge in God's promises and my own prayer takes flight: "My hope is in you, Lord. Renew me. Help me to soar on wings like eagles, even if they are metal ones that race me to my next destination. Help me to serve those I meet on the way."

I think of Paul growing weary on his journeys. He may have had fewer babies to contend with, but he endured weeks of grueling travel and months in stark prison cells. I'm sure his bread and water would make airline food seem like a gourmet feast. But still he persevered, looking to the Lord for the strength he needed to continue his work.

Instead of wallowing in complaints about overcrowded or delayed flights, I need to keep my perspective—"Hey, it's still faster than covered wagons!" Like Paul, let us all hope in the Lord and renew our strength.

Lord, help me to be a tireless servant of God using talent on loan from you. Plug me into your uplifting power. Let me soar in service.

Terry Paulson

An Open Seat to Peace

In the hustle and bustle of preparing for business on the road, we often find ourselves fighting a case of the "tudes" . . . as in attitude! Conflict has a way of sneaking in to steal the serenity we try so hard to maintain.

One such time for me came on a cold December night with the first winter snow of the year. With my flight canceled, I had two options: (1) fly out the next day or (2) fly to Orlando and take a bus over to Tampa. With a business engagement the next day, I had to get to Tampa. I opted for the trip to Orlando and frantically scurried to make the flight that was about to depart.

As I settled into my seat on the plane, which was now at full capacity, the little four-year-old girl sitting between her mother and me must have sensed the stress on the part of all the relocated passengers. Without looking up from her artistic endeavor in a coloring book, she said to me, "Sorry you had to get stuck sitting next to a little kid." What a stress buster!

God honored his Word—perfect peace in the midst of flight changes, weather challenges, and inconveniences— because I trusted in him. He even gave me a great little girl for a seatmate!

 Lord, thank you for your promise of perfect peace. Help me to understand that in all situations it is your gift to me when my thoughts are focused on you . . . a very small price to pay for such a precious gift.

Lori White

The Painful Process

I have been crucified with Christ. Galatians 2:20

Christ's crucifixion is the source of our hope. Yet the thought of the pain and agony associated with crucifixion is troubling; the thought of us experiencing crucifixion is terrifying. But Paul says we have been crucified with Christ. What does that mean?

Many would embrace the feel-good aspects of the gospel and ignore the real cost that Christ paid for our salvation and redemption. Many tenets of New Age thought are attractive because they promise something for nothing: Hang a crystal from your rearview mirror and it will magically channel goodness into your life.

Although the gift of salvation is free, the cost of following Jesus is great. It is easy for us to deny that to live as Christians we must be continually crucified to the desires of sin.

I once shared with a fellow traveler how frustrating it is for me to try to live a victorious Christian life and to repeatedly make the same mistakes. If I have been crucified with Christ, why do I continue to commit the same sins? My friend shared a story.

An elderly lady was counseling a younger believer who posed the same question. The wise elder replied, "You forget, my child, that crucifixion is a long, painful process."

We gladly share in Christ's victory, but do we also embrace his suffering? Are we willing to resist sin, reject old habits, and deny the flesh? To experience true Christianity, we cannot have one without the other.

 Lord, resisting sin is painful. Comfort me as through the power of your Son I daily crucify the temptations and evil desires that would defeat me.

Mark Sanborn

Perilous Times

But know this, that in the last days perilous times will come.
2 Timothy 3:1 NKJV

These are perilous times. Travel is fraught with perils beyond even those we face at home. The physical peril—irresponsible cab drivers, inexperienced pilots, rental cars driven in unfamiliar areas—is less threatening than the spiritual peril. The evil one delights in our spiritual demise, and he will stop at nothing to achieve it.

How do you deal with the perils of the road? I once read about a study of pastors who had remained faithful and avoided the pitfalls of sexual lust and infidelity. One thing they shared in common: None of them believed it couldn't happen to them. What? Let me repeat that in a different way: They all believed they were vulnerable to sexual temptations. The pastors who fell victim to sin were often those who said, "It will never happen to me."

The lesson for us is clear: We must acknowledge the spiritual peril that awaits us. We must know that none of us is superhuman, that only through our acceptance of our own weakness and dependence on God's strength can we hope to emerge from the battle unscathed.

Perils await even you. You are not immune to temptations or their devastating consequences. But by depending on God's strength, you can live wisely in these perilous times.

God, my protector, it is plain that I live in perilous times. The evil of the world threatens me physically and spiritually. Let me not deny nor discount the peril of the times, but neither let me surrender to it because your strength and protection are greater. Keep those I love safe in your protection, especially when I am away.

Mark Sanborn

The Pilot

When I consider your heavens, the work of your fingers, the moon and the stars, which you have set in place. Psalm 8:3

The flight attendant's voice came over the intercom: "Ladies and gentlemen, welcome to flight number 403 service to Columbus." As we prepared for departure, I heard the too often "please fasten your seat belts and follow the safety card . . ." I closed my eyes, tired. I wished I were heading home. My thoughts were interrupted by the flight attendant's voice. "And now a special word from the pilot."

"Good afternoon, Tim. Please take a moment to say hello to the person next to you. Take your nose out of your paper and look into the eyes of the people around you. Some of them are hurting. Listen. I do it for you when you make time for me. You've been asking for signs of my work. Look out the window at the sky. I've painted a sky splashed with a variety of colors. Below you the ground is an intricate creation, carved out of a mass of earth. Flowers, trees, streams, lakes, and rivers dot the countryside. Be still and know that I am with you . . ."

The plane bumped and I was startled. I sat up and rubbed my eyes. I had been praying for God to show me his presence. I smiled at the flight attendant, looked out the window, and saw the beauty of an incredible sunset. "Thank you, God," I prayed. "Help me to see you in still, small moments of each day." I turned to my seatmate and began an adventure-filled conversation.

 Dear God, help me to open my eyes and ears each day.

Tim Richardson
(Adapted from *Jump Starts: Words of Wit and Wisdom to Supercharge Your Day,*
1999 by Tim Richardson, edited by J. Lenora King)

A Prayer Meant to Be Sung

Glory to God in the highest. Luke 2:14

There is something about an early morning walk on an empty beach that helps me adjust to time zone changes when I'm on the road. This morning I saw pieces of driftwood that looked like rafts on the slow-moving waves. The shiny, broken shells that were worn by waves long past caught my eye in shallow pools. I found myself focusing my attention on the wonder of just being alive. As I picked up my pace to a jog, a song slowly emerged—strands woven like the small pieces of seaweed kissing the foam.

80

> Every day sacred. Every day holy. Fresh gift from God.
>   Light of new dawn. Praise the new day!
> Open my eyes to the lessons it brings.
> Let my heart learn the songs I must sing.
> Give to my heart the wisdom to see
> The way I might serve all living things.
> Every day sacred. Every day holy. Fresh gift from God.
>   Light of new dawn. Praise the new day!
> In work may I use what talent I bear.
> In play may I laugh and smile so to share.
> In rest may I pause and listen anew.
> In love may I show to all that I care.

Like the early church that lived and breathed the psalms, my heart craves music of the soul. Who needs a radio when God can play the chords?

Lord, thank you for music and the gift of song that helps my heart soar no matter where I travel. Keep playing the music, Lord.

Eileen McDargh

Price for Privilege

For unto whomsoever much is given, of him shall be much required.
Luke 12:48 KJV

Upon arrival at the Geneva airport, I was told that my confirmed business class seat on my flight to the United States was now in jeopardy due to overbooking. After a long trip, I was exhausted and needed more room than coach class afforded. So I pleaded with the airline agent . . . and I prayed. Minutes later, my prayer was answered.

My priority was to sleep on the flight, but God had another plan. After reading my Bible for a few minutes, the gentleman next to me asked if I always read the Bible or only when flying. This prompted a lengthy conversation about my faith in Jesus Christ and his belief in God. He was a Muslim who had been educated at a Christian school, and he admitted he didn't really know what to believe. He made the comment, "As long as you believe in God, it really doesn't matter what your faith is." Then he looked at me and said, "You probably don't agree."

I smiled and explained that in the Bible, which Christians believe to be the Word of God, Christ says, "I am the way, the truth, and the life: no man cometh unto the Father, but by me." Although I couldn't recall the Scripture reference, I miraculously opened my Bible to John 14:6 and showed him the text. As we parted, I assured him that God would reveal the truth to him if he would simply ask.

The business class seat was more than a blessing to me; it was a divine appointment to speak to a searching soul.

 Dear Lord, thank you for all you have given me. Let me always use your blessings for the furtherance of the kingdom.

Lori White

A Purpose for Every Trip

And this gospel of the kingdom will be preached in the whole world as a testimony to all nations, and then the end will come. Matthew 24:14

I've found a way to make work a thrilling adventure instead of merely a necessary drudgery. You can turn your job into, as the Blues Brothers would call it, "a mission from God!" It's simple, yet it will change your life dramatically if you are willing to let God guide you and to act when prompted by the Holy Spirit. Here's what you do. Put five gospel tracts in your briefcase, pocket, or purse and pray for God to show you whom to give them to, where to leave them, or with whom to share them. You will be absolutely amazed at the people the Lord will place on your heart.

Every area of your life will be transformed. You will look at people differently: "Is she saved?" "I wonder if that man needs an encouraging word?" "Could I be the one to share Jesus with this customer?"

God will never push you to do something you aren't capable of, but he will stretch you if you are willing. He will bless you beyond words if you will only climb out on a few spiritual limbs for him.

Let's face it, I am challenging you to do the most frightening thing most people could ever imagine: Share your faith.

Dear Lord, I know you will guide me only where you know I can make a difference and only into situations that I can handle. I'm going to start trusting you today to use me. Thank you for never leaving nor forsaking me.

Bill Sanders

Put Your Luggage Where Your Faith Is

Where your treasure is, there your heart will be also. Matthew 6:21

If you're like me, as a true road warrior you pride yourself on your ability to travel light. Everything is miniature. Everything has its place. And if something isn't essential, it's soon left behind. Like pioneers of old, road warriors are good at making those tough choices about what to take and what to leave behind. This practice stands in marked contrast to the way we collect things at home—closets full of clothes we seldom wear, expensive furniture, toys and equipment we seldom use. Only visitors seem to notice and admire our great stuff. Being a road warrior shows you what you actually need to make the journey through life.

I wonder what Christ and his apostles carried with them as they walked the roads of Galilee as road warriors of old? What did they take with them to stay plugged into the power of their faith? If what we carry on the road speaks to what is important to us, I'm not sure anyone would know we are Christians. Maybe it's time we put our luggage where our faith is. We could start by making room for a small Bible and this devotional.

Lord, there is much that I possess that isn't important, clutter that some would call treasure. I confess that much is there to impress rather than to serve. Help me to make room in my traveling essentials for your Word, the spiritual guide I so often fail to read. Help me to set aside space in my luggage and time in my day for letting you reach me.

Terry Paulson

Raisin Bran or . . . Lovely Thoughts!

Whatsoever things are true, whatsoever things are honest, whatsoever things are just, whatsoever things are pure, whatsoever things are lovely, whatsoever things are of good report; if there be any virtue, and if there be any praise, think on these things. Philippians 4:8 KJV

Is it so difficult to deliver raisin bran with fruit and skim milk in a reasonable amount of time? Is it so difficult to tell the truth when asked when the order left the kitchen? "It just left" means twenty more minutes of waiting! Don't they understand that this is all I ask to bolster my sleepy body to a point of passion for my calling? Then the gentle voice of your Word, Lord, races into my brain, my heart, my soul: Think on these things—whatsoever things are true, honest, just, pure, lovely, of good report, virtue, and praise.

Why is it so easy to become distracted by what appear to be urgent things in life and bypass the things of eternal value? Why do my stomach's growl and my need for physical satisfaction make me forget my focus on faith and the heavenly truths that bring peace?

I forget I can't be to others what I am not.

I forget that God is the source of my joy, peace, and beauty.

I forget how hungry we all are for more than temporal food.

And I forget he is here—in the room, recognizing my frustration and waiting for me to relax in his peace.

Lord, reverse my early morning eagerness to rush through a routine. Let me stop a moment for a sunrise, a visit with you, a prayer, and a time to "think on these things." Thanks for waiting for me.

Naomi Rhode

Rent That Cart!

Cast all your anxiety on him because he cares for you. 1 Peter 5:7

Arriving at gate 36 and departing on a connecting flight from Gate 5 is usually no problem because of the airport tram system. But the tram system was not working. And because I *thought* I was traveling light, I didn't bring my luggage wheels.

At first, the thirty-one-gate hike didn't seem too bad. It felt good to walk after sitting on a three-hour flight. Besides, my carry-on load didn't feel too heavy. But the farther I walked, the heavier it got! My pace slowed . . . considerably.

Yes, there were plenty of luggage carts for rent, but for some reason I kept thinking I could make it to my gate, and I continued to pass up the opportunity to ease my load.

I arrived at gate 5 aware of every aching muscle, and I questioned my sanity. Why didn't I rent a cart? Was it the cost? pride? stubbornness? Whatever it was, I was now paying the price.

I wonder how many other loads I have carried needlessly. How many times has my Father offered to ease the burdens of my heart, but I have chosen to carry my load alone. It costs so little to give it all to him, and yet I stubbornly hang on to the weight and pay dearly for my foolishness.

How it must grieve God's heart to see his burdened children choose to ignore his outstretched arms of love.

Father, forgive me for the times when I have insisted on carrying my own load. Open my eyes to your comfort and presence. Help me to let go of my stubborn pride and let you be my "cart" of strength.

Gail Wenos

The Resort of Solitude

Be still, and know that I am God. Psalm 46:10

I remember the resort. It was located in a beautiful wooded area far from any city, and my travel plans required that I arrive a day before for my presentation. After wheeling my luggage into my room, it hit me. What?! No TV? No *Headline News?* How was the world going to get along without me knowing what was happening? I explored the room further. More bad news—no phone or Internet jack for my computer! This was no resort; it was more like a prison.

Slowly I realized there was no place to go, and I was trapped with myself . . . in silence. I learned something about myself and about solitude that day. You don't make silence; you enter into what is always there. I had gotten comfortable with noise and distractions in my life. My hotel room TV was often on for background noise. My computer connection to the Internet provided a constant reminder of a to do list that wouldn't go away. But this time there were no distractions I could create.

In the silence of solitude, great things from God grow, and they often grow deep. This particular day was a Sunday, and I had not had time to attend services because of my early morning flight. I sat on my bed and pulled out the Gideon Bible. God and I had time together that afternoon. My prison was turned into a prism that reflected new patterns of God's light into my room.

God, help me not to wait for forced silence. Help me to turn off the noise and take advantage of stillness each day that I might grow deeper in you!

Terry Paulson

Road Rage and Unexpected Blessings

Bless those who persecute you; bless and do not curse. Romans 12:14

I didn't think I had cut him off, but even if I had, there was no excuse for him riding my bumper. To avoid further problems, I got out of the fast lane and offered a quick prayer for the man as he passed. I was still unsettled by the rage I saw in his face when I took my seat on the flight. I talked about it with the young professional sitting next to me. As I shared my experience, he showed me a headline in the paper: "Road Rage." More and more drivers are taking out their anger on America's highways.

As men of faith, we talked about anger and how easy it is to let anger rule. He told me about a recent business trip and a confrontation he had in a Mississippi country bar. He was the only black person in the bar, and he was surrounded by locals. One man said, "We don't want your kind in here." My traveling companion said he saw a cross peaking out from the man's open shirt, so he made eye contact and said as warmly as he could, "As a fellow believer, if you beat me up, I'll remember you for as long as it takes me to heal. If we talk and share a drink together, I have a feeling we'll remember each other for as long as we live."

There was a long pause and a cautious smile before the words came. "Then I take it you're buying!"

The encounter cost my companion a few dollars, but it was a conversation he would remember for a lifetime. To hate another is to be a prisoner of that hate. Through faith let us trade curses and anger for prayers, dialogue, and a heartfelt blessing.

 Lord, free me from hate so I can be free to love.

Terry Paulson

Seeing through God's Eyes

If any of you lacks wisdom, he should ask God, who gives generously to all without finding fault, and it will be given to him. James 1:5

My favorite definition of *wisdom* is seeing things through God's eyes. God's perspective is a radical departure from what I tend to see. When I'm on the road, I check my interpretation of situations by asking, "What does God see?"

I might see unfriendly people in a restaurant. God sees people who hurt.

I see the water of an ocean. God sees his handiwork.

I often see employees in the hospitality industry who don't seem to care. God sees lives he can infuse with new enthusiasm and commitment.

My sight settles on a mean exchange of words between strangers. God sees an opportunity for redemption.

I see people who seem odd, and in their differentness, threatening. I am humbled when I realize God sees children he loves every bit as much as me.

Charles Handy said, "Change the way a man thinks, and that changes everything." Perhaps the way we think begins with what we see.

Lord, give me your perspective. Help me to look with different eyes and view the world as I travel with the compassion of Christ. Show me the common experiences of life with uncommon insight. Let my wisdom be not of the world but of you.

Mark Sanborn

Seizing the Day for Joy

This is the day the LORD has made; let us rejoice and be glad in it.
Psalm 118:24

Pastor Bob Lawson has had a great impact on my Christian life. Every day, at the end of his early morning run, he sings the doxology to the sunrise to keep fresh the reality of God's gift of another day. My neighbors are probably thankful I never followed that example, but the gift of joyful song has never been far from my memory.

For years I have also been impressed with Southwest Airlines and their innovative ways of bringing surprise to their low-budget, high-fun flights. Many of their flight-attendant teams are known for singing a comical closing message. During an invigorating conversation with a fellow Christian sitting next to me, I shared Bob Lawson's joyful habit. And so when the Southwest flight attendant launched into song, I decided it was time for this traveler to risk singing back an appropriate response. Doing my best revised version of a *Sound of Music* classic, my loud tenor voice took flight to a surprised plane. "So long. Farewell. Auf wiedersehen. Good-bye. With fares like this who needs a lousy meal. Good-bye. Good-bye. Good-bye!" The laughter and applause were appreciated and I'm sure were in no way indicative of the quality of the singing! The head flight attendant invited me to stay on the plane for the next leg as part of her team. I thought to myself, "When I became a man, I put away childish things . . . like the desire to just get old and act grown up!"

Seize every moment God gives you for its unique novelty. Don't depend on scheduled joys. God works in moments not in years.

 Lord, thank you for the gift of moments and the spirit of joy that lets me enjoy each one.

Terry Paulson

The Shepherd Cares for His Sheep

Yea, though I walk through the valley of the shadow of death, I will fear no evil. Psalm 23:4 KJV

My shoulders and neck ached, not from the weariness of the travel but from the fear I was experiencing. Johannesburg, South Africa, is a beautiful, thriving city, but the atmosphere is charged with the sense of being "under siege."

My host had suggested we go to the local shopping district for bagels and cream cheese. She parked her BMW, and as I opened the car door, I was greeted by a man on horseback carrying a machine gun. My friend JoAnne explained that car theft occurred every seventeen seconds, and the military police were attempting to curb that problem.

As we approached the shopping area, JoAnne reminded me to secure my purse. Purse snatching was a game here she said.

When we returned home, the gigantic wrought iron gates at the entrance to the driveway opened electronically. I noted the barbed wire on the top of the stucco wall and saw the iron bars on the windows and doors of this gorgeous home, and I remembered that we had locked the iron doors inside the house between the living room and the bedroom when we had gone to bed the night before.

I could not wait to board the flight back to Phoenix that evening. Once safely seated in business class I began to relax. Only then did the reality dawn on me. The Shepherd alone is in charge of the sheep's safety. Every place he leads us is equally safe! I had ignored the reality of his protection, thus my stress and tension.

 Dear Shepherd, please help me to see my daily experiences as coming from your hand instead of so often viewing things from an earthly perspective.

Glenna Salsbury

Some Suffering Optional

In all these things we are more than conquerors through him who loved us. Romans 8:37

If you had asked me five years ago whether I liked to travel, I would have replied emphatically, "I hate it!" But that was before I heard a talk given by my friend Jim Pelley. Jim was giving a presentation to a group of speakers, and he said, "I hear speakers say they don't like to travel. I suggest they either quit traveling, or they choose to like it." Jim's words hit home with me.

You are a road warrior; you travel out of necessity. It is part of what you do for a vocation. And travel can be difficult and tiring. But has the drudgery of travel conquered your spirit?

You can choose to enjoy travel. Instead of focusing on the negatives, focus on the benefits: the time to do uninterrupted work, a chance to get caught up on your reading, opportunities for stimulating conversations, the potential for meeting new friends and expanding your network of business contacts, and plenty of time to focus your thoughts on God.

Improving the quality of your road experiences begins with a choice. Make it a positive one.

Lord, I've been guilty of some negative thinking about life on the road. At times I've chosen to focus on the pitfalls and have ignored the possibilities. Remind me that I don't need to suffer unnecessarily. I pray for the ability to choose to make travel the best experience it can be for myself and those I come in contact with.

Mark Sanborn

Someone Is Watching

Do not set foot on the path of the wicked or walk in the way of evil men. Avoid it, do not travel on it; turn from it and go on your way.
Proverbs 4:14–15

It is, in my opinion, more difficult to live the Christian lifestyle we profess when on the road because wrong things are easier to do: It is easier to "preview" the in-room movies with adult themes . . . easier to chew out the front desk clerk for an injustice, real or perceived . . . Seldom does anyone observe us getting off course and hold us accountable to get back on track. On the road, it seems as if nobody is watching.

Of course, someone is watching. We become so preoccupied with our external appearances that we forget that the most important observer is our heavenly Father. He sees our indiscretions, and they hurt him.

You've probably heard people referred to as "Sunday Christians." Maybe there are also "home-based Christians." These people live out their faith only in the community of family and friends. Their real desire is spiritual respect from others rather than obedience to the living God. But God demands our obedience twenty-four hours each day, and to that I add, whether at home or on the road.

Lord, I know you are watching at all times because you love me and want me to walk in obedience to you. Remind me daily how my actions appear to you. I want to serve you all the time—at home and on the road—so that my actions are always pleasing to you.

Mark Sanborn

Standing at the Crossroad

Do not put the Lord your God to the test. Matthew 4:7

As road warriors, we stand at the intersection of temptation every day. Just as Jesus Christ was tempted by the devil, the evil one, we are bombarded by media images and enticing choices intended to take us down the wrong road. We must remember the responsibility of being in a city or town away from our loved ones and colleagues and step up to the challenge of our faith. As Winston Churchill said, "The price of freedom is constant vigilance." We, too, must strive to be vigilant to remain free from the snares of sin.

Don't take the first step down the path to destruction. When tempted, think of your brother and sister road warriors. Pray for them to be strong, and through your conscious contact with God, you will stay on the narrow but safe path.

The ultimate reward is the spiritual strength you gain by staying faithful to the Spirit buried in your heart and soul. This glory you will share with others as you pass by and when you return to hearth and home. Pray for the warriors who become weak and are tempted that they may return to the righteous way. Give thanks to the Lord. The Lord gives to you no more than you can carry.

 Lord, the devil, the evil one, tempts me in many delicious ways, urging me to take negative actions that lead to guilt and pain. Through my faith in you, Lord, my spiritual armor will repel the devilish tricks. Keep me close to your love and care.

Bob Sherer

Strange Parking Lots, Dark Streets, Long Hallways

I am the light of the world; he who follows Me shall not walk in the darkness, but shall have the light of life. John 8:12 NASB

Today, traveling alone in America can be a fearful experience. Do you remember as a child living in a country where doors were left unlocked? We walked to school without any hesitation, and we smiled easily at strangers.

This morning I returned from a nine-day trip to six different cities. My jogging shoes were used only twice this trip because of the caution of hotel advisors to stay inside. Each hotel had a list of safety warnings—warnings to use the peep hole or to ask for an escort to walk you to your room if you were alone.

I returned to Phoenix in time to hurry to our morning church service. I opened the bulletin and read the title of the sermon: "How Great a Light." What a marvelous contrast. What hope after the darkness of strange city streets and hotel hallways. Amid the reality of our age, the message of Jesus addresses our hearts and fears. "I am the light of the world! You won't walk in darkness when you walk in my light!"

Do these promises excuse carelessness or remove my need for diligence and common sense? Of course not. All through Scripture we are exhorted to be wise, prudent, and aware of danger, but not out of fear, and certainly not out of the deepest darkness of all: the darkness that exists without the presence of the indwelling Spirit of God.

 Father, you are the Light of the World. You dwell in me. Give me boldness and courage to go and be a light to the world! Send me fearlessly because you go with and before me.

Naomi Rhode

The Sun

He gives strength to the weary and increases the power of the weak.
Isaiah 40:29

Yesterday was a tough travel day! I put on some sweats and slowly walked down to the beach in front of the ocean-front hotel where I'd be speaking later. My travel schedule was beginning to get to me. I longed to be home. As I lamented about my situation, I looked up. In the west was a yellowish white globe that was now ducking down on the horizon. In the east, a globe of a different color was about to make its presence known as it began to peek over the awesome waters of the Atlantic Ocean. It was fantastic. I stood on the beach mesmerized by this awesome event and then remembered my problem. I put my head down as if the weight of the world were on my shoulders.

There was a flash in the east! The sun broke through. A moment ago it was out of sight, but now it was an incredible ball of fire that would light the sky with radiant color and warm the day. The moon, now disappearing, was becoming more and more faint as the sun rose. I felt the presence of God on this Maundy Thursday morning in an incredible way. I also learned a valuable lesson: The darkness in my life, like the moon, will soon disappear with the coming of a new day. It is that new day that I must look forward to and not at past challenges or problems. Each day we are given a chance to start over with a fresh new perspective.

 Dear God, help me through challenges and lead me to enjoy the many ways you bless me.

Tim Richardson
(Adapted from *Jump Starts: Words of Wit and Wisdom to Supercharge Your Day,*
1999 by Tim Richardson, edited by J. Lenora King)

Supernatural Horizon

Set your minds on things above, not on earthly things. Colossians 3:2

"Two prisoners looked through prison bars; one saw mud, the other stars." Which prisoner are you most like?

Flying reminds me that no matter how bad the weather is on the ground, someplace higher above me, the sky is clear. It is always an amazing sight when an airplane breaks through a dreary, rainy cloud layer and suddenly the sky is illuminated by sunshine. In such instances, we have truly "risen above."

Our minds are that way. How we "set our minds" determines our perspective. Today before leaving for the airport at 6:00 A.M. I tried to log on to America Online to check my business e-mail. As is often the case, I was frustrated then angered by the host computer's inability to service my request. I had wasted valuable time and was now running late. As I hurriedly drove to the airport, suddenly my coffee splashed through the tiny hole in the lid and stained my new shirt. Needless to say, my mind was set "below" not above when I finally reached the airport.

Pilots use an instrument that creates an artificial horizon. It shows them where they are in relation to the earth below. Likewise, God provides us with a spiritual horizon that shows us where we are in relation to him and his heavenly kingdom. We must continually check our spiritual instrumentation to see if we have set our minds above or on our earthly problems below.

Lord, keep my perspective focused on your truth. Fix my eyes on you and your Son. Send your Holy Spirit to show me the things above, and help me to choose to set my mind on your desires for me.

Mark Sanborn

Supreme Sacrifice

Just as the Son of Man did not come to be served, but to serve, and to give His life a ransom for many. Matthew 20:28 NKJV

I always thought I understood the sacrifice God made when he offered Jesus as a substitution for my sins. But I never understood it fully until my wife, Darla, and I had our first child.

Hunter was born in the second year of our marriage. It was an incomparable blessing for me to be in the delivery room when he entered this world. Early on, Hunter experienced some problems that not all babies face. In addition to colic, he had gastrointestinal reflux, a very painful condition for the little guy. When it didn't improve, we took him to see a specialist.

Our hearts ached at the discomfort the medical tests caused our child. My wife and I would gladly have suffered for him—taken any pain and discomfort from him and experienced it in his place. The thought of allowing others to torture him—humiliate him, beat him, spit on him, and then nail him to a cross—my mind cannot comprehend! The pain would be too much to endure!

And yet that's what God did. He gave his only Son, because the only thing he loved as much as Jesus was us. You and me. What an amazing love the love of God is.

Lord, I can scarcely imagine how much you love me when I consider that you sacrificed your own Son. The pain you endured as your Son suffered must have been heartbreaking, but I know your heart was already broken over my sins, and that's why you let Jesus pay the price to bring me into a right relationship with you. Thank you for your amazing love.

Mark Sanborn

Sweet Fellowship

That ye also may have fellowship with us: and truly our fellowship is with the Father, and with his Son Jesus Christ. 1 John 1:3 KJV

There is a loneliness that comes with being on the road. There are times when you experience loneliness in a hotel room, in an airport terminal, or on a flight, even when someone is sitting next to you. Those are the times you need and want sweet fellowship.

When you establish a rapport with your heavenly Father, you experience a comfort and a fellowship so sweet they defy description. He desires our communication and is willing and able to fill the void in our lives. He wants to commune with us more than we can imagine.

Today, with all the ease and availability of modern communication, it still doesn't rival the simplicity of communication and fellowship with our wonderful Creator and Lord. Not to mention, the rates are cheaper and you will never have a bad connection or get a busy signal.

First thing in the morning, as you're clearing away the cobwebs, make a spiritual connection. During your day, stop for just a moment, say thanks, and then learn to listen for God's still small voice. Last thing at night before putting your road weary bones to rest, open the communication lines once again. You can enjoy the sweetest fellowship on earth when you make a heavenly connection.

God, I love those times of sweet fellowship with you. I'm reminded of your care, your concern, and your great love for me. Thank you for being patient with me when I forget to open up the lines with you.

George Hendley

Taking a Daily Leap for Joy

Rejoice in the Lord always. I will say it again: Rejoice! Philippians 4:4

All road warriors have their share of bad days: The hotel shuttle comes *when*? What telephone access charges? I never opened the minibar! I owe what? We've already been delayed two hours! Are they building a new plane?

When faced with potholes in the road, I sometimes struggle to recover my sense of joy. I temporarily join the ranks of the "frozen chosen," those terminally serious believers who seem to think God's children should not have to experience life's travails, and then let their faces show it. It's easy to forget that no matter what the circumstances, joy is one of the fruits of the Spirit!

Happiness depends on what happens to you—it's a function of circumstances that can change from day to day. Joy defies circumstances and is a choice made by faith through God's grace. Claim God's promise of joy every day! Send a note to a fellow road warrior: "Until further notice celebrate every day as a gift from God!"

In Luke 6:23, Jesus challenges us to "leap for joy." The next time you need a lift in a crowded airport, try a spontaneous leap for joy. Click your heels, and watch the smiles emerge. Since you have to be with yourself all day long, you might as well claim joy as your companion.

 Lord, help me to claim your power and perspective on every journey and let one of my constant companions be your joy!

Terry Paulson

Tears and Prayers for a Stranger

Jesus wept. John 11:35

It seemed like just another cross-continental flight from LAX to Orlando. Suddenly there was a scurry of activity. Ten rows back, the ashen face of the man slumped in the aisle seat said more than any of us wanted to hear. There was frantic action and CPR in the aisle. I, like many others on the plane, began to pray for a man I did not know. We made an unscheduled landing in Texas, and the man was taken off the plane. We never heard whether he survived.

God never said we would not experience tragedy in life, and none of us knows when we may be called to face it. Does God care when tragic events happen? He does care, and he feels our pain with us. Knowing that Jesus wept reminds us that we are never alone.

We can minimize pain by avoiding life, but we are called by faith to live boldly. We can avoid loss by avoiding love, but we are called by God to love anyway.

Being a person of faith doesn't guarantee a perfect, painfree life, but it does mean we can claim God's loving support whenever it is needed.

Lord, thank you for being with me during the ups and the downs, the victories and the tragedies, and for weeping for me and with me on my journey.

Terry Paulson

Temple Maintenance

Do you not know that your body is a temple of the Holy Spirit, who is in you, whom you have received from God? You are not your own; you were bought at a price. Therefore honor God with your body.
1 Corinthians 6:19–20

Our bodies are temples of the Lord, but judging from the condition many of us are in, especially those of us who travel, *shacks* might be a more appropriate term. I've often wondered if Christ—were he traveling today as we are—would work out on the road. My conclusion is that he would have done what was necessary to protect the sacredness of his earthly temple.

Of course he didn't need to work out during his travels. Jesus and his disciples walked, they didn't fly. They slept on floors and hard ground, not king-sized beds. They ate for sustenance, not pleasure. Necessity, not luxury, guided them.

I enjoy good meals when I travel, but years of experience have taught me to make dessert an exception rather than the rule and to make time for exercise. It isn't easy, but it is necessary to keep my temple in good repair.

We are to be stewards of all God gives us, not the least of which are our bodies. Although the condition of our souls is to take priority, being a road warrior does not abdicate us from caring for our bodies.

Lord, teach me to prioritize my time and energy to maintain the health and physical condition necessary to serve you and live fully. Make me mindful of what I eat and how much exercise I should get not only when I travel but when I'm home as well. Remind me that I am a steward of this earthly temple.

Mark Sanborn

Thirsty

Like newborn babies, crave pure spiritual milk, so that by it you may grow up in your salvation. 1 Peter 2:2

Babies are beautiful, but you know that those sweet little infants can become cranky and downright demanding when they're hungry. When they want milk they will fuss, whimper, and even scream until they get it. And you may have one nearby on your flight right now!

How many of us thirst for the Word of God like that? How often do we become spiritually dehydrated because we don't regularly drink from the Scriptures?

The above verse paints a vivid picture of the thirst and desire we are to have for Scripture, and the objective is clear: growth. We cannot grow without reading the Word just as a newborn cannot grow without the nourishment of milk.

When our son Hunter was a newborn, he wanted to nurse every two to three hours, and sometimes even more often. He woke up regularly even in the deep of night to eat. Biologically programmed to grow, he needed ongoing nourishment!

How often do we give up the nourishment of the Word when we travel? Do we become scripturally malnourished on the road? We should have the continual craving for Scripture that an infant has for milk. A little time spent on the airplane, in the back of the cab, while waiting for an appointment, before retiring each evening—these times can bolster our "single feeding" in the morning. Learn to crave the Word as a baby craves milk.

Lord, make me thirsty for your Word! I desire to grow, so remind me to drink of the Scriptures more often each day. Create in me the same desire and need to read and study Scripture that a newborn has for milk.

Mark Sanborn

Too Busy

He will reply, "I tell you the truth, whatever you did not do for one of the least of these, you did not do for me." Matthew 25:45

He began talking to me about needing money for something to eat. *I was hungry and you fed me. I was thirsty and you gave me something to drink.* His story sounded like one he had used countless times before, I reasoned as I walked on telling myself that I helped out the needy through my volunteer work at the local soup kitchen. A few "I will work for food" signs made little impact on me or the few other business professionals walking in the same direction.

It was a cold day and steam was coming out of the manholes. A fire in a trash can warmed a few hands but probably no hearts. *I was naked and you clothed me. I was sick and you visited me.* As I walked on, I heard soft crying and then I saw a sign that told a story about job loss, apartment eviction, and HIV infection. If I only had time to get involved, I thought. *I was in prison and you came to me.* I arrived at my hotel and checked into my room. As I opened the desk drawer to get the room service menu, I saw the Gideon Bible. *When you do this to the least of my brethren, you have done this unto me.* I bowed my head and wept.

Dear God, it is easy to bypass others in need in the busy life I lead. Please help me to take time to comfort a stranger, to love someone who feels unloved, and to help the helpless.

Tim Richardson

Trading In My TV Party

Your word is a lamp to my feet and a light for my path. Psalm 119:105

One of my goals is never to need to buy shampoo again. It's a goal that only another road warrior could understand. Free shampoo is one of those little perks associated with travel. Another is cable TV. Our TV is seldom on at home, but on the road the TV fills the cold, isolated room with sound. It's the cheapest way to have a party because you don't have to pay for room service to feed anyone. And if I don't like one party crowd, I can click my way to another. I guess I am a traveling "bed potato."

But in the drawer next to the bed is that ever ready Gideon Bible. It doesn't require a flashy remote to access its insight and power, and I will not be charged for the right to unleash the joy that resides within its pages. We all have silly habits on the road that waste time we could be spending growing in our faith. On the road, there are new roads to take and many unfamiliar paths to walk. Reading God's Word provides the light that can guide my every step. I wouldn't travel without a map. I shouldn't risk taking the wrong turn because I forgot to turn on God's lamp.

Lord, help me to trade my TV habits for time growing closer to you. Steady my thoughts on meaningful prayer. Give me the wisdom to open that drawer and the desire to read your Word so that you can shine your light on my path.

Terry Paulson

Traveler's Alert

Be on the alert, stand firm in the faith, act like men, be strong. Let all that you do be done in love. 1 Corinthians 16:13–14 NASB

At the beginning of each year, I choose a few verses to guide me on this new journey—a new year—verses to steer my decisions as I face the empty pages of my yearly planner. There will be miles to add to my frequent flyer account, journeys filled with stress and distress, new places, people, and opportunities. I need a focus.

This year my key verses have been 1 Corinthians 16:13–14.

The warning: "Be on the alert." I must be alert and avoid the spiritual danger of not being who I say I am and not maximizing my gifts for the benefit of others.

The challenge: "Stand firm in the faith," when it would be easier to follow the world's standard of conduct.

The admonition: "Act like men" (and women) who are born anew because of Christ's death and redemptive power.

The expectation: "Be strong" in the strength of the Lord, when temptation is blatant and perspective is easily lost.

The encouragement: "Let all that you do be done in love." What an awesome world mine would be, Lord, if I and others were encouraged to do everything with kindness and love.

These should do's are my traveler's alert for this year! They are holding me in good stead on my journey because the reward is for now . . . and forever!

 Father, thank you that you cared to give me a warning, challenge, admonition, expectation, and encouragement all in one verse. I love having your Word as my focus.

Naomi Rhode

Traveling Companions

Let us not give up meeting together, as some are in the habit of doing, but let us encourage one another. Hebrews 10:25

Isn't it amazing to find brothers and sisters in Christ wherever you go? In the years I have been traveling, one of the real surprises of the Christian life has been the bond that is forged with people I meet who love and worship the Lord—people in different cities, in different denominations, who worship in ways I do not usually worship, but who are part of the body of Christ universal.

I have found these people in a beautiful church in Cambridge, England, in an open air charismatic chapel in Maui, Hawaii, in an inner city church in Manhattan, and in a large Southern Baptist church in Atlanta. The music, the order of service, the social standing, and attire vary. The Scriptures read, the communion celebrated, the prayers offered, and the light that shines through true believers are the same!

One of the most memorable experiences of worship I had took place in Shanghai, China. The great cultural revolution in China tried but failed to kill this shared faith, this love for Christ. What a thrill it was for us to rise early on a rainy day, take two trolley cars, and walk down a long alley to find believers—two thousand believers singing in Chinese, "Living for Jesus!"

It is impossible to keep believers from assembling together! We find each other, even if it is a casual gathering at one of our business meetings. What a thrill it will be in heaven some day to say, "Don't I know you from somewhere? England? Maui? New York? Atlanta? Oh, yes! China!" Traveling companions and friends in the Lord forever.

Lord, I celebrate the body of Christ in every corner of your world. Thank you for letting me find your traveling companions everywhere I travel.

Naomi Rhode

Truth-Centered Living on the Road

If you abide in My Word—hold fast to My teachings and live in accordance with them—you are truly My disciples. And you will know the truth, and the truth will set you free. John 8:31–32 AMP

Everyone has his or her opinion of truth and what it is. Jesus Christ said, "Sanctify them . . . by the Truth. Your Word is Truth" (John 17:17 AMP). God's Word gives us solid ground on which to face life on the road.

Truth is not subjective nor a relative decision made by arbitrary means or analysis. Truth, like science and math, has a precision and an exactness to it that cannot be argued. It goes beyond the realm of facts. Unlike facts that can change from moment to moment, truth is unchanging.

If we want to live the truth, we should go to the fountainhead of truth: God's Word. The Bible, although scoffed at and considered ancient history by many, is the source of truth-centered living. This Book of Life gives us the truth and direction for life whether we are at home or on the road. If we want God's opinion and his answers to life's many questions, we can go to his road map for our journey.

Truth-centered living is built on the foundation of a knowledge and belief in the truth. To know the truth is the greatest knowledge. To live the truth is the greatest achievement. Learning to live out the principles and precepts in the Bible is the greatest challenge with the greatest rewards. Take time on the road to find the wisdom and power that come from God's Word.

Heavenly Father, you have given me your Word as a signpost for living, as a road map for life. Thank you for the simplicity of your Word and your loving encouragement to make it my rule book for life.

George Hendley

An Unknown Soldier Goes Home

God loves a cheerful giver. 2 Corinthians 9:7

So many people with open hands come at you when you're on the road. Some approach you at the airports wearing ministerial collars you're sure are not authentic. Still others, claiming they have lost their wallets, approach you at the baggage area asking for money to get home. Do they have the face of Jesus? I have no way of telling. I have given money to people claiming need. Some plead, "I'll pay you back." I always reply, "There is no need to pay me back. Give it to someone you meet who needs it as you did today." But do my random acts of kindness make a difference or just support bad habits of good con men?

One Sunday, I was changing flights in Chicago. I was on my way home for the holidays, so I found a bank of phones to let my wife know I was halfway home. As we talked, I overheard a young soldier leaving a message from the next phone. "Mom, they won't change the ticket without more money. I don't have it. I'll try to stay here by the phone. Please call me at . . ."

"How much do you need, soldier?" I asked.

"Sir, I'm twenty dollars short of getting home."

"Young man, there are times I have given money to people I wasn't sure really needed it. For giving to our country, I am honored to give you this twenty dollars. Now, go home."

That day an unknown, young soldier and a middle-aged traveler experienced a blessing at a bank of pay phones. Praise God for the gift of giving.

 Lord, thank you for your grace. Even though it seems you get taken advantage of by sinners, you keep giving and loving anyway. Help me to do the same.

Terry Paulson

Upgrade to First Class

Do not let any unwholesome talk come out of your mouths, but only what is helpful for building others up according to their needs.
Ephesians 4:29

Not that airline again! My demeanor changed when I was greeted at the counter pleasantly with, "Good afternoon, Mr. Richardson!" I walked away feeling good, a smile hovering around my mouth. I thought to myself, "I really should have told that woman how much I appreciated her kindness and understanding," so I returned to the counter and told her that she was probably the nicest agent I'd ever met. It felt good giving a compliment.

There is a certain euphoria that comes in genuinely, sincerely giving someone positive feedback. As I approached the tarmac, an attendant stopped me. "Excuse me, are you Mr. Richardson?" he asked. "You have a seat assignment change. You've been upgraded . . . to first class."

My smile returned, the chuckle bubbled up again. "Yes, thank you, I know," I said.

"But you couldn't have known, sir," the attendant persisted. "The change was just radioed down."

I grinned, calling over my shoulder as I mounted the steps to the plane, "I know, but you see, I upgraded someone else and that upgraded me."

The poor boy didn't have a clue as to what I was saying, but I did. I had been upgraded to first class already, and it had nothing to do with my seat assignment.

Dear God, help me daily to look for the good in others and for opportunities to give a kind word or a sincere compliment.

Tim Richardson
(Adapted from *Jump Starts: Words of Wit and Wisdom to Supercharge Your Day*, 1999 by Tim Richardson, edited by J. Lenora King)

What a Deal I Have for You!

We brought nothing into the world, and we can take nothing out of it.
1 Timothy 6:7

In those last few minutes before landing, I love to browse through the airline gift catalogs for those things I just must have as a road warrior. There's the traveling answering machine that handles the messages I can't live without, the collapsible golf putter with porta-hole, and the tacky tie shade that protects silk ties from messy airline meals. The many gadgets remind me of a bumper sticker I saw once: "He who dies with the most toys . . . still dies."

What treasures really matter most in life? I choose the priceless memories of people. I treasure moments with family and friends, but as a road warrior, I also value the countless encounters with people I have met on my many journeys. I recall that man in Paris who put up with my high school French to give me needed directions. There was Brother Clarence, who moved to the window seat so I had room for my luggage and then went on to help me understand how God can get you to the ripe old age of ninety-nine. I remember countless other ready smiles and inspirational verses shared by men and women I can only remember by face.

As usual, I close the catalog, decide to pass on the tie shade, and try a last minute conversation with my neighbor. What treasure will I find there today?

 Lord, thank you for the priceless gift of people who grace my journey today. Help me to appreciate the treasures of faith and experience they have to share.

Terry Paulson

What Do I Have to Offer?

Man looks at the outward appearance, but the LORD looks at the heart.
1 Samuel 16:7

The morning was hectic. Calls, interruptions, details . . . all needing to be dealt with before I left to speak at a business luncheon. Then I encountered heavy traffic and red lights, and I made two wrong turns. I arrived . . . frazzled!

Walking in and looking around, I noticed how everyone looked so together, so businesslike. I thought, "Lord, help! What can I possibly have to offer them?"

While trying to regroup, I could almost hear my Father saying, "Look again. Underneath all that togetherness are hurting hearts. Stop comparing yourself with others. Just be yourself, and let me do the rest."

Those words of assurance settled into my heart, and I realized that my Father had already gone before me to prepare the way. Shaking hands and looking into the eyes of individuals, it became obvious that there was a lot of pain in that room.

How often do we miss opportunities to touch hurting hearts because we are intimidated by someone's position in the corporate structure? How often does someone's outward appearance make us feel that we have nothing to offer them? We all know about "doing unto the least," but what about the others? Some of the loneliest people are the ones at the top.

Father, there are times when I forget that I am a child of the King, and I focus on my feelings of inadequacy. Give me the eyes to see beyond the outward appearances and to see instead the hearts that so desperately need your touch of love.

Gail Wenos

Whistle while You Work

Our mouths were filled with laughter, our tongues with songs of joy.
Psalm 126:2

I had been on the West Coast all week and was more than ready to come home. I took the red-eye flight leaving San Diego at 12:35 A.M. In addition to the discomfort of traveling all night, there was a three-and-a-half-hour layover in Atlanta. My weariness coupled with the inconvenient layover affected my attitude. I began to complain as I talked to myself. "I want to be home. I'm tired of traveling all the time. Why isn't there an earlier flight?" I had definitely allowed my situation to take control of my attitude.

I walked into a rest room in the Atlanta airport at about 5:00 A.M. and was greeted by loud singing. I didn't see anyone and was curious, so I looked around. Finally, I found a middle-aged man singing as he cleaned a toilet. I certainly was impressed that he was singing, but I was even more impressed when I realized what he was singing. The song I heard loud and clear was "Don't Worry, Be Happy!"

There in the men's room on a Sunday morning, God gave me a little sermon I needed to hear. If this man could find joy in a job thought by many to be degrading, certainly I could find joy in a career filled with so much . . . even when I had to travel to some inconvenient places at some inconvenient times.

 Dear God, help me to be enthusiastic in my life and to share my enthusiasm and love for you with everyone I meet.

Tim Richardson

Who Are You Praying For?

Therefore I exhort first of all that supplications, prayers, intercessions, and giving of thanks be made for all men. 1 Timothy 2:1 NKJV

We are called to pray for everyone, even the people we don't like—like the front desk clerk who was unhelpful or the guy who barged in front of you in the check-in line. What could you possibly pray about for them?

You might think that praying for God to fix them would be a good start. But maybe they aren't broken. Maybe the front desk clerk is new and frustrated by a lack of training. Perhaps the guy who barged in line just learned that his wife had been in a car accident and was trying to catch the first flight to be with her.

God knows the needs of each heart even when you and I don't. We can pray for God to meet the needs in the lives of those we encounter, but we can also pray for understanding. We need God to work in our lives to help us understand others as he does. The character of God, especially as revealed by his Son, Jesus Christ, indicates that God feels the pain of the sinner before he feels the pain of his or her sin.

Pray for everyone. And pray that you might understand them as God does.

 Father, it is easy to pray for those I love; it is difficult to pray for those I dislike. I am easily offended by others, but I forget the pain my own offenses cause. I pray for the needs of those I encounter today and for the ability to better understand them and the ways they hurt.

Mark Sanborn

Worshiping with Those Other Christians

Do not judge, or you too will be judged. Why do you look at the speck of sawdust in your brother's eye and pay no attention to the plank in your own eye? Matthew 7:1, 3

After reading in the paper about the latest report of a controversial ecclesiastical action, it's tempting to wonder how people in *that* denomination can even call themselves Christians. Welcome to the "I'm fine—you're defective" wing of the Christian faith. Unfortunately, we are around Christians who are like us entirely too much. They share our taste in liturgy, hymns, and favorite verses. As a result, we may begin to assume that God has ordained our way of worship as the one and only way of expressing faith. From a distance it is easy to judge the faith of others, but as road warriors, we get to experience and be touched by other Christians up close and personal.

There is one family of God called to celebrate together a risen Lord. As a Christian who travels for a living, I have been blessed with the chance to worship in different lands with men and women who share the Christian faith. I've shared a prayer with an Amish family, passed candles with babushkas in a Russian Orthodox cathedral, started singing too early in Westminster Abbey, and listened for a word I could understand in a Swedish sermon. Each worship service provided a unique window into the kingdom of God. May we judge less and celebrate our common faith more.

Lord, turn my critical eyes inward so I may grow in grace and understanding. Purify and perfect my own walk of faith so that I may be a living witness to others. Transform my quick judgments of other Christians into prayer, understanding, and service.

Terry Paulson

About the Editors

Known internationally as "the high content speaker who motivates," **Mark Sanborn** presents an average of one hundred programs a year on leadership, teamwork, change, and customer service. His audiences include Fortune 500 companies, associations, and churches. In 1995 he was inducted into the Speakers Hall of Fame. He is the author of the books *Teambuilt: Making Teamwork Work* and *Sanborn on Success,* as well as numerous videos and audio training programs. He and his wife, Darla, lead a couples Bible study in Denver, Colorado. To receive a free publication about Mark's learning resources and programs, contact him at 1-800-650-3343 or http://www.marksanborn.com.

A psychologist, professional speaker, and author of *They Shoot Managers Don't They?, Making Humor Work,* and *Secrets of Life Every Teen Needs to Know,* **Dr. Terry L. Paulson** provides practical and entertaining programs for corporations and associations that empower leaders and teams to make change work. *Business Digest* calls him "the Will Rogers of management consultants." He is the 1998–99 president of the National Speakers Association and an enthusiastic tenor in his church choir. To receive information about his programs and a free article about change, contact him at DrTerryP@aol.com, www.changecentral.com, or 818-991-5110.

Contributors

He is called husband, dad, brother, son, minister, speaker, trainer, author, friend, leader, and some names that aren't appropriate to print. **George Hendley** is all that and more. But the title that he cherishes most is child of God. George works with organizations that want to serve people and leaders that want to grow people. His presentations on leadership, listening, and change give a variety of audiences fresh insights, practical information, and hope for the future. Contact him at 972-234-4377 or ghpresen@wans.net.

As author of *Work for a Living and Still Be Free to Live* and a contributor to business journals and newspapers, **Eileen McDargh** travels the globe keeping audiences stimulated and laughing with her Performance Mastery programs. Called a "human capitalist," she draws upon practical business know-how, life's experiences, and over twenty years of consulting to national and international organizations. Her audiences discover how to create spirited work and home environments "by design and not by default." Contact her at McDargh@aol.com, www.eileenmcdargh.com, or by calling 714-496-8640.

Naomi Rhode is an inspirational keynote speaker and author of *More Beautiful than Diamonds: The Gift of Friendship, The Gift of Family: A Legacy of Love,* and coauthor of *Speaking Secrets of the Masters.* Naomi speaks on leadership, empowerment, teamwork, and communication skills. She is vice president of SmartPractice, serves on corporate boards, and is the past president of the National Speakers Association and winner of its highest honor, the Cavett Award. Contact her at nrhode@smarthealth.com or 1-800-522-0595, ext. 214.

Tim Richardson is a full-time professional speaker and coauthor of *Transformation Thinking*. He recently completed his second book, *The Breakfast of Champions*. He is a Certified Speaking Professional (CSP) and a former IBM employee. He speaks to corporate and healthcare clients on the topics of balance, change, and success by choice not by chance. In addition to his keynote presentations, Tim is a certified ropes course facilitator. He can be reached at 904-249-0919, Tim RichCSP@aol.com, or www.TimRichardson.com.

Recognized for her wisdom, enthusiasm, and high energy, **Glenna Salsbury** is featured nationally and internationally on the platforms of corporate gatherings, association programs, and Christian retreats. Glenna's presentations focus on finding purpose in the midst of change and improving communication among customers, employees, and teams. Glenna served as the 1997–98 president of the National Speakers Association and is the author of *The Art of the Fresh Start* and the popular audiotape series *Passion, Power and Purpose*. You can contact Glenna at ISpeak4U@aol.com or 602-483-7732.

Bill Sanders speaks to 250,000 teens and parents each year in school assemblies and parenting sessions. Audiences love his warm blend of humor, storytelling, and sincerity. He is the author of fourteen books and two *Chicken Soup for the Soul* stories. His latest parent book, *Seize the Moment, Not Your Teen,* has been turned into a twelve-week video series. Contact him for information and a free tape at 8495 Valleywood Lane, Portage, MI 49024-5257, billtalks@aol.com, or 616-323-8074.

A former Fortune 500 executive vice president and author of *Doing the Right Thing, The Ultimate Profit, Fear: The Corporate "F" Word,* and numerous articles, **Bob Sherer's** keynote addresses and workshops focus on the "people side of quality." He's known as the performance plus speaker, and his coaching and strengthening of communication skills contribute to improved performance, productivity, and profits. Generously giving his time to prison work, Bob challenges convicts to face responsibility and embrace spiritual commitment. Contact him at http://www.qualityconcepts.com or 1-800-545-3998.

A "million miler" with the airlines, **Gail Wenos** is a seasoned road warrior. A member of the National Speakers Association, Gail markets herself as a humorist. With the help of her special associate, Ezra D. Peabody (a dummy), she brings messages of teamwork and making a difference to corporations, associations, and churches across the nation—messages that touch the heart and change lives. For further information contact Gail at Gailnezra@aol.com or 714-771-1166.

Known as a change-of-pace speaker, **Lori White** has a unique way of conveying timely messages by using ventriloquism, music, and humor in her customized presentations. With a background in telecommunications and international hotel sales, her areas of expertise include interpersonal communications and sales/marketing. Lori is an ambassador of hope determined to make a difference in a world beset by constant change, rejection, and absence of understanding. Feel free to contact her at LoriWhite@aol.com, 1-800-733-2690, or P.O. Box 250, Pigeon Forge, TN 37868-0250.

Index

abstinence 78, 93
acceptance 21,
46, 56, 73, 85,
91, 113
action 23, 57, 63,
65, 83, 101,
105, 111
adoration 15, 16,
20, 21, 79, 80,
95
adversity 21, 24,
36, 37, 54, 59,
73, 74, 76, 77,
91, 93, 96, 99,
112
ambassadors 18,
26, 48, 55, 66,
72, 81, 103, 108
anger 54, 68, 87
anxiety 36, 37, 51,
76, 90, 94

beauty 79, 80
belief 19, 22, 26,
30, 41, 42, 44,
45, 49, 64, 71,
77, 81, 82, 98,
105, 114
Bible 32, 35, 42,
49, 60, 65, 81,
83, 102, 105,
107
blame 68
blessing(s) 15, 16,
20, 21, 25, 28,
32, 34, 43, 47,
84, 85, 89, 95,
109, 110, 112
boasting 57, 63,
85, 114
busyness 30, 39,
45, 52, 54, 62,
69, 84, 103, 104

calling 18, 22, 26,
48, 49, 50, 55,
61, 66, 72, 81,
103, 111
caring 40, 48, 52,
66, 70, 74, 97,
100, 103, 108,
109

cheating 78, 92
children 25, 39,
45, 47, 62, 76,
97
church 106, 114
comfort 75, 100,
103, 108
companions 52,
64, 71, 100,
106, 110, 113
complaints 51,
59, 91
conduct 18, 29,
48, 55, 64, 70,
72, 92, 93
conflict 68, 71, 87
courage 36, 37,
65, 71, 93
courtesy 24, 70
conversion 26,
28, 41, 44, 81,
82

deadlines 37, 39,
62, 76, 84

disappointment 34, 59, 73, 99

duty 18, 23, 26, 48, 55, 58, 66, 72, 81, 82, 101, 103, 108

exhaustion 17, 51, 75

failure 34, 77, 92

faith 19, 22, 26, 30, 36, 38, 45, 49, 60, 61, 63, 64, 81, 88, 96, 98, 107

faithfulness 19, 27, 50, 61, 71, 78, 92, 93, 105

family 39, 45, 47, 56, 62, 64, 67, 97

fear 17, 51, 90, 94

forgiveness 29, 34, 68, 70, 87, 113

generosity 21, 40, 43, 66, 70, 103, 108, 109

gratitude 21, 25, 40, 43, 67, 79, 109, 112

guilt 34, 77, 92, 93, 103

health 23, 58, 74, 101

honesty 22, 49, 69

hope 15, 20, 44, 56, 66, 73, 82, 90, 94, 95, 100

hospitality 24, 25, 40, 43, 48, 52, 55, 70, 109, 110

humility 29, 57, 78, 111, 114

humor 71, 89, 112

immorality 92

immortality 28, 41

integrity 18, 55, 57, 72, 93

joy 17, 47, 58, 80, 89, 99, 112

judgment 68, 71, 87, 114

justification 29, 50, 77

loneliness 17, 33, 51, 67, 94

love 28, 39, 41, 45, 48, 62, 64, 67, 97, 105, 113

moderation 101

paradise 16, 28, 41, 56, 86

patience 37, 38, 59, 63, 75, 76, 84

peace 17, 35, 51, 54, 75, 84, 86, 90, 94

perfection 29, 77

plan 26, 42, 46, 56

power 15, 20, 35, 65, 75, 95, 105, 107

praise 27, 47, 80, 89, 99, 112

prayer 19, 30, 33, 36, 37, 98, 100, 113

prejudice 57, 68, 87, 114

pride 31, 57, 85, 111, 114

procrastination 69

promise 16, 46, 60, 63, 104, 105, 107

purpose 22, 31, 49, 50, 53, 61

quiet time 32, 35, 86, 98, 102, 104

refuge 32, 106
repentance 29, 77
revenge 68, 87
riches 53, 83
rushing 54, 86

safety 36, 78, 90,
    94
salvation 16, 44,
    77, 82
self-confidence
    33, 50, 65, 111
self-control 23,
    38, 63, 68, 78,
    87, 92, 93, 101
serenity 35, 63,
    73, 75, 86
service 18, 40, 43,
    48, 52, 55, 57,
    58, 66, 70, 72,
    74, 103, 108,
    109, 111

success 31, 34,
    38, 41, 47, 50,
    53, 61, 63, 65
surrender 29, 42,
    46, 63, 78, 85

temptation 77,
    78, 92, 93
testimony 16, 18,
    22, 26, 28, 41,
    44, 48, 49, 55,
    64, 71, 72, 81,
    82
thanksgiving 16,
    21, 24, 25, 27,
    32, 40, 43, 79,
    80, 89, 99, 109,
    112
time 35, 39, 45,
    53, 62, 69
tolerance 68, 70,
    87, 113, 114

travel 47, 56, 91
trust 19, 24, 36,
    37, 42, 46, 59,
    63, 73, 76, 111
truth 42, 107

unbelief 44

vision 15, 20, 88,
    95, 96, 105

wisdom 42, 60,
    73, 88, 96, 102,
    104, 107
work 31, 50, 66,
    91, 111
worship 106, 114
worry 17, 24, 36,
    37, 51, 54, 76,
    90, 94, 100